TECHNICAL AIR INTELLIGENCE CENTER

REPORT #41

JAPANESE BALLOON AND ATTACHED DEVICES

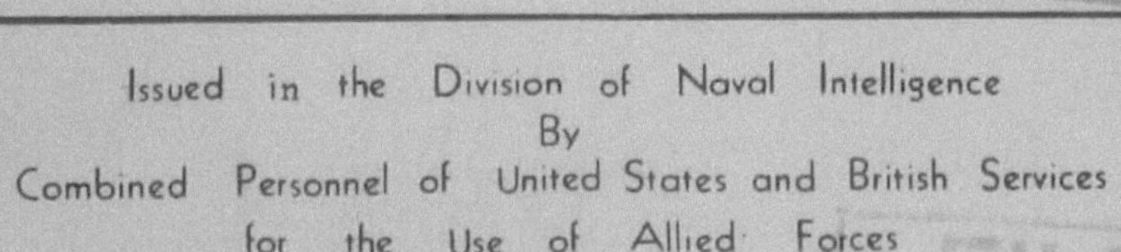

Issued in the Division of Naval Intelligence
By
Combined Personnel of United States and British Services
for the Use of Allied Forces

TECHNICAL AIR INTELLIGENCE CENTER

NAVAL AIR STATION ANACOSTIA D C

ISBN 978-1-304-82297-0

OPNAV-16-V No. T241

TAIC REPORT NUMBER 41

May 1945

JAPANESE BALLOONS AND ATTACHED DEVICES

ISSUED IN THE DIVISION OF NAVAL INTELLIGENCE
BY
COMBINED PERSONNEL OF UNITED STATES AND BRITISH SERVICES
FOR THE USE OF ALLIED FORCES

TECHNICAL AIR INTELLIGENCE CENTER
NAVAL AIR STATION
ANACOSTIA, D. C.

DISTRIBUTION LIST ON LAST PAGE

Introductory note

This report represents the results of tests conducted on the various parts of Japanese Balloons that have been submitted to the Technical Air Intelligence Center for examination. There has, in this report, been no effort to evaluate the various aspects of the subject, but merely to present the material in a readily usable form to facilitate any studies that might be made.

In order that there be more accurate reporting of the material found, the reporting form was created. It represents the combined effort of the Military Intelligence Service of the Army and the Office of Naval Intelligence of the Navy, but is in no sense final, and constructive criticism both as to content and form is welcome. It is easily recognized that the use of the form will result in more accurate transmission of information.

The composite table was created from every source available and since the reports were, in many cases, in conflict with each other, the resulting information may not be accurate in all cases and it is requested that any additional information that is now, or becomes available be transmitted, through channels, to the Army or Navy Agency in Washington that is appropriate.

It is contemplated that the reporting form and the explanatory notes be published in a restricted volume in the event it is requested by interested agencies.

INDEX

SUGGESTED REPORTING FORM

BOMB INCIDENT____
BALLOON INCIDENT____

STATE OR PROVINCE____
REPORTING OFFICER____
DATE OF INCIDENT____

PLACE OF INCIDENT____
UNIT____
DATE OF REPORT____

1. Envelope or part thereof recovered____
2. Number of plies of paper____
3. Thickness of paper____
4. Number of gores____
5. Width of gores at widest point____
6. Color of paper____
   Color of seams____
7. Is envelope destructor standard____
   Is it meant to be used____
8. Type of envelope destructor fuse____
9. Length of envelope destructor fuse____
   Burned____ Unburned____
10. Number of shroud lines____
11. Material and size of shroud lines____
12. Type of valve____
13. Valve marking____
14. Valve number____
15. Valve pressure____
16. Type of shock absorber____
    Indicate presence of shroud lines____
    Support ropes____
    Shock absorber____
17. Is ballast release gear standard and if not indicate difference____
18. Is battery present____
    Is battery standard____
19. Fluid around battery present____
    CaCl or what other solution____
20. Pairs of unblown plugs total____
    Location____
21. Single unblown plugs total____
    Locations____
22. Is aneroid assembly standard____
    If not describe____
23. Setting number one____
24. Setting number two____
25. Setting number three____
26. Setting number four____
27. Is ballast gear release destructor used____
    Is it standard____
    Location____
    If not describe____
28. Wiring diagram A__ B__ C____
    If other describe and diagram____
29. Number of arming wires or evidence of them____
30. Number of sandbags____
31. Weight and location on ballast ring____
32. Number of incendiary bombs____
33. Type and location on ballast ring____
34. Number of H.E. Bombs____
35. Type and location H.E. Bombs____
36. Number at top of envelope____
37. Disposition of material____
38. Remarks____

Additional data source and date____

JAPANESE PAPER BALLOONS

In order to more uniformly report and catalogue incidents connected with Japanese paper balloons the form which follows these explanatory notes has been created. The columnar explanations show past experience and any deviation should be fully described. The use of the form which follows and the reporting form will facilitate later analyses and make trends more readily apparent.

Column 1. (fig. 1) Envelope

The following letters are used to report, in general terms, the condition of the envelope.
R - Rubber
F - Fragment
SD - Shot down
B - Burned or exploded

From Japanese sources it has been determined that the diameter of the envelope is 33.3 feet (10.15 meters), although reports of examinations have indicated other dimensions.

Column 2. Number of plies

The number of plies has been found to be four or five of long fiber paper.

Column 3. Thickness

The thickness of a given sample of five plies was found to vary between .0075 and .009 and four plies vary between .006 to .0072

Column 4. Number of Gores

The number of gores is determined by counting the strips on either side of the center line of the balloon. (Note in fig. 1 that the gores do not run continuously from top to bottom.)

Column 5. Width of gores

Width of gores is measured from center of seam to center of seam at the widest part of the gore. (Near the equator)

Fig. 1

Column 6. Color

There have been reported three different colors of balloons. These are noted in column 6 by the letters A, B, and C.
A - Light tan with light tan seams
B - Light tan with blue seams
C - Bluish white with bluish white seams.

Column 7. Envelope destructor Fig. 2

The envelope destructor is a paper sack containing 250 grams (8.7 ounces) of magnesium flash powder and is cemented to the envelope above the cantenary band.

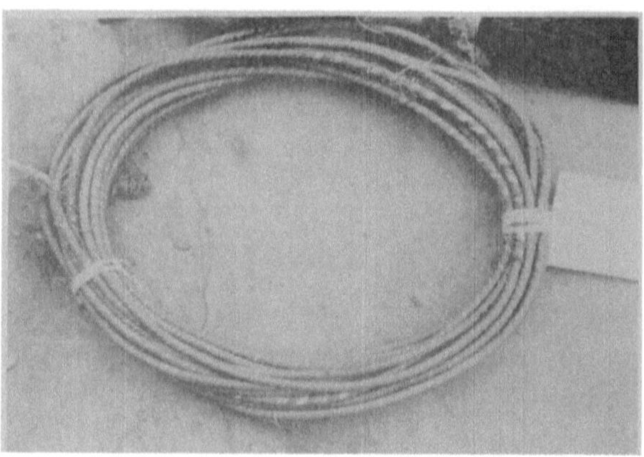

Fig. 2

Fig. 3

Column 8. Type of envelope destructor fuze. Fig. 3

A - This is the only type fuze so far found. It is a paper cord fuze that burns at the rate of approximately one foot in 66 seconds.

Column 9. Length of envelope destructor fuze

This measurement includes both the burned and unburned portions.

Column 10. Number of shrouds

All balloons so far reported have had 19 shroud lines. These have all been reported as being about 38 feet long.

Column 11. Type of shrouds. Fig. 4.

A - Only one type of shroud line has been reported to date. These are three strand, nine thread manila hemp, $\frac{1}{4}$ inch in diameter. (The shroud lines are differentiated from the support ropes attached to the ballast release gear. The support ropes are usually 3/8 inch in diameter.)

Fig. 5

Type A

Column 12. Fig. 5 and Fig. 6. Type of valve.

The valves reported are made from .041 inch thick metal with an outside diameter of 19.5 inches. The valve opening is 17 inches in diameter. There are two types.

A - Fig. 5. This type has flat supports and a rather elaborate pressed pattern in the diaphram.

B - Fig. 6. Has pressed ribbed supports and simple circular pattern pressed into the diaphram.

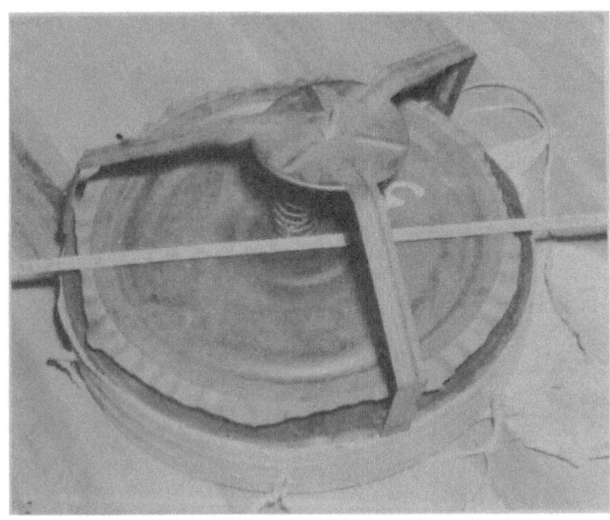

Fig. 6

Type B

Column 17. Fig. 8. Ballast gear.

Fig. 8 represents the standard ballast gear and any deviation from this should be noted, such as the placing of the ballast gear demolition block under the aneriod housing, etc. This will be designated as A.

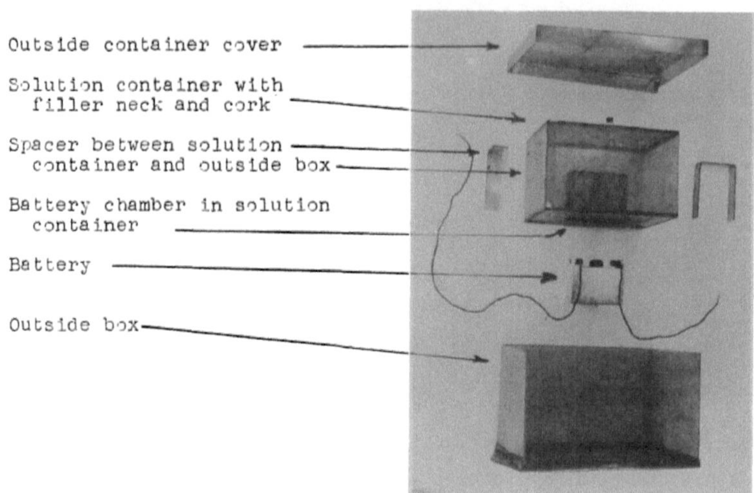

Fig. 9

Column 18. Fig. 9. Battery

The battery is a one cell wet battery which contains a sulphuric acid electrolyte. It has five plates and when fully charged is rated at approximately 2.2 volts.

Column 19. Calcium chloride solution.

The solution has been reported as a ten or twenty percent solution of calcium shloride. Where known the percentage should be shown as well as the use of other solutions.

Column 20. Blow out plugs type. Fig. 10 and 11

A - This type is a machined iron plug with cross-hatch knurl

B - This is a permanent mold plug with straight knurl

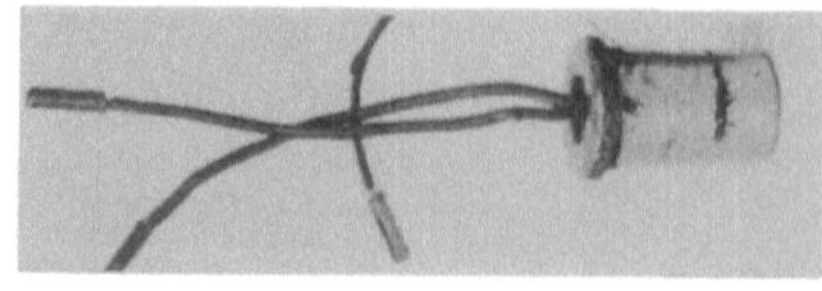

Fig. 10. Type A

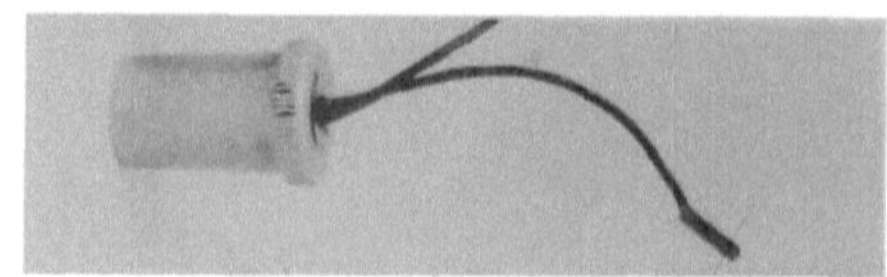

Fig. 11. Type B

Column 20. Pairs of unblown plugs. Total

Column 21. Single unblown plugs. Total

Fig. 12

Column 22. Aneroid type. Fig. 12

A - As shown in Fig. 12 with all units covered
B - As shown in Fig. 12 with some units uncovered - no covers for some units
D - As shown with all units covered but with one painted with a triangle or delta

Column 23. Setting of number one aneroid
Column 24. Setting of number two aneroid
Column 25. Setting of number three aneroid
Column 26. Setting for number four aneroid (Clutch aneroid)

Column 27. Ballast gear destructor Fig. 13

The ballast gear destructor is a $2\frac{1}{2}$ pound block of picric acid in a metal container. (Also shown in Fig. 13 is the detonator)

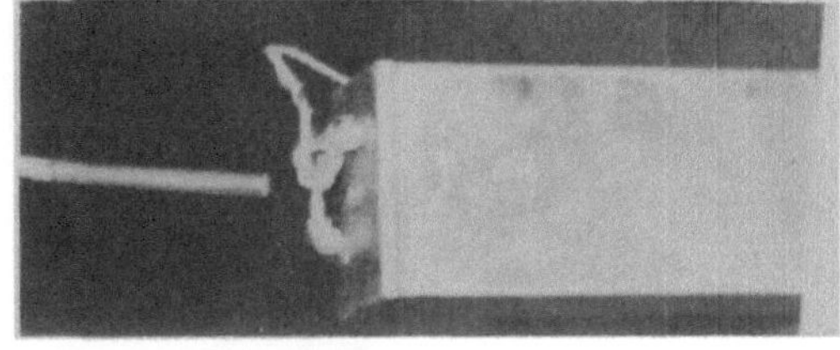

Fig. 13

Column 13. Marking on valve.

Indicate how the marking was accomplished as follows:

A - Stamped into the metal in letters about ¼" high
W - Painted in white paint
Y - Painted in yellow letters

Column 14. Numbers on valve.

Column 15. Pressure valve is set to operate.

This can be expressed as ounces per square inch, pounds per square inch, or inches of water necessary to open.

Column 16. Rubber shock absorber. Fig 7.

Only one type has so far been found and this type is not found on all balloons It is made up of 250 strands of 3/64 inch rubber bands held in a woven cotton cover at the ends. It is 22 inches long with ten inches of rubber exposed. A load of 100 pounds will cause the sister rope to become taut.

Fig. 7

Fig. 8

Column 28. Wiring diagram

A - Wiring diagram
Figure 14.

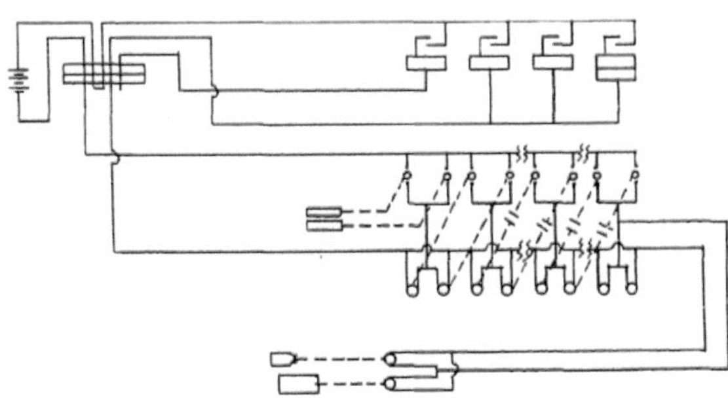

B - Wiring diagram
Fig. 15.

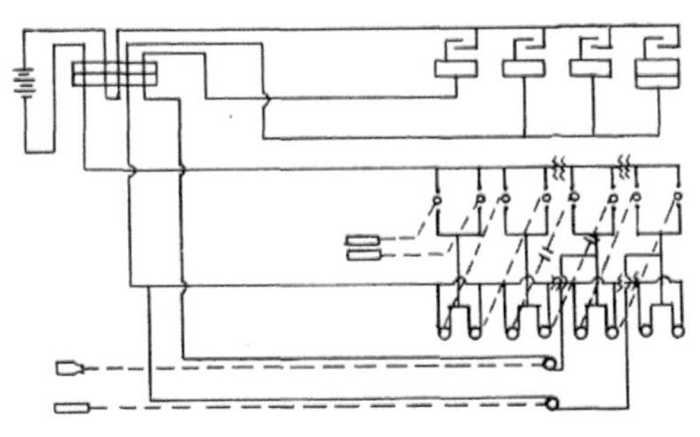

C - Wiring diagram
Fig. 16.

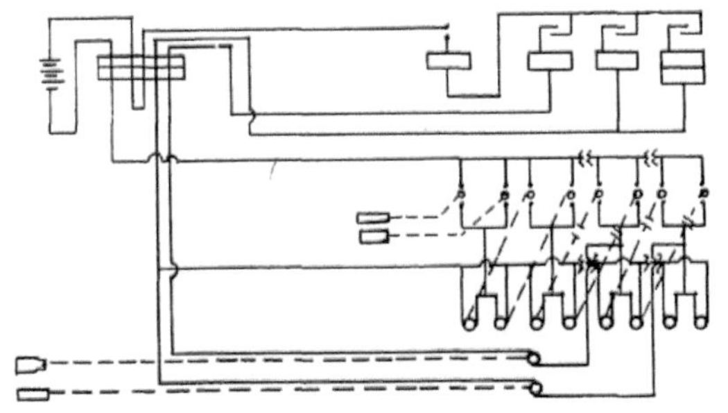

Column 29. Arming wire, number of. Fig. 17

Note any indication of arming wires whether the wire is still attached or there is only the cord usually attached to it.

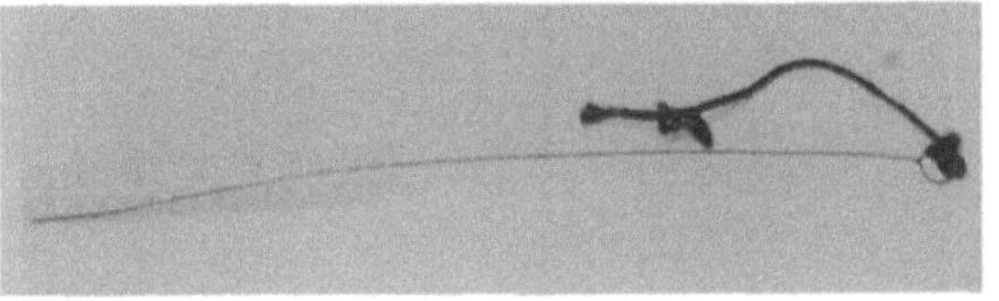

Fig. 17

Column 30. Number of Sandbags
Fig. 18.

Column 31. Weight of sandbags
Fig. 18.

Where more than one sandbag is found note the weight of each sandbag at the bottom of the form, and the number of the plugs to which it was attached.

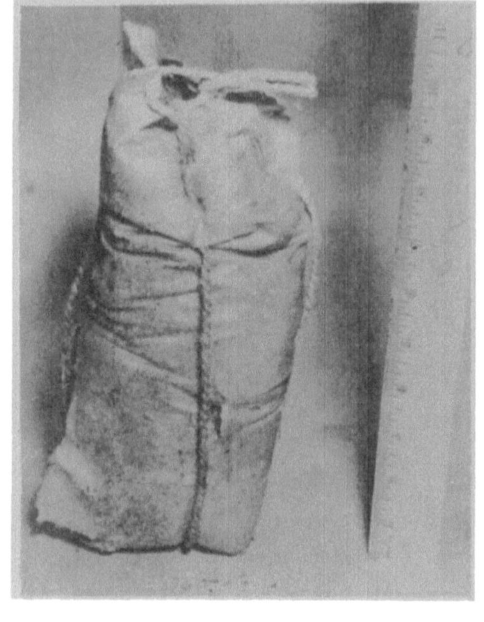

Fig. 18

Column 32. Number of Incendiary Bombs. Fig. 19 and 20   Fig. 21 and 22

Column 33. Type of incendiary bomb. Fig. 19, 20, 21, and 22.

A - 12.8 Kg. Incendiary Fig. 19 and 20

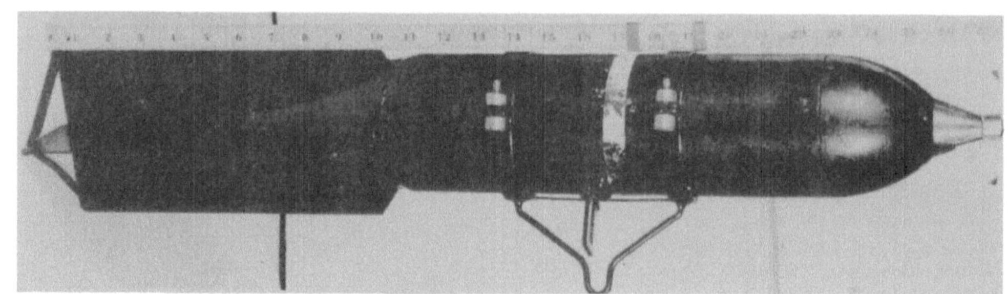

Fig. 19

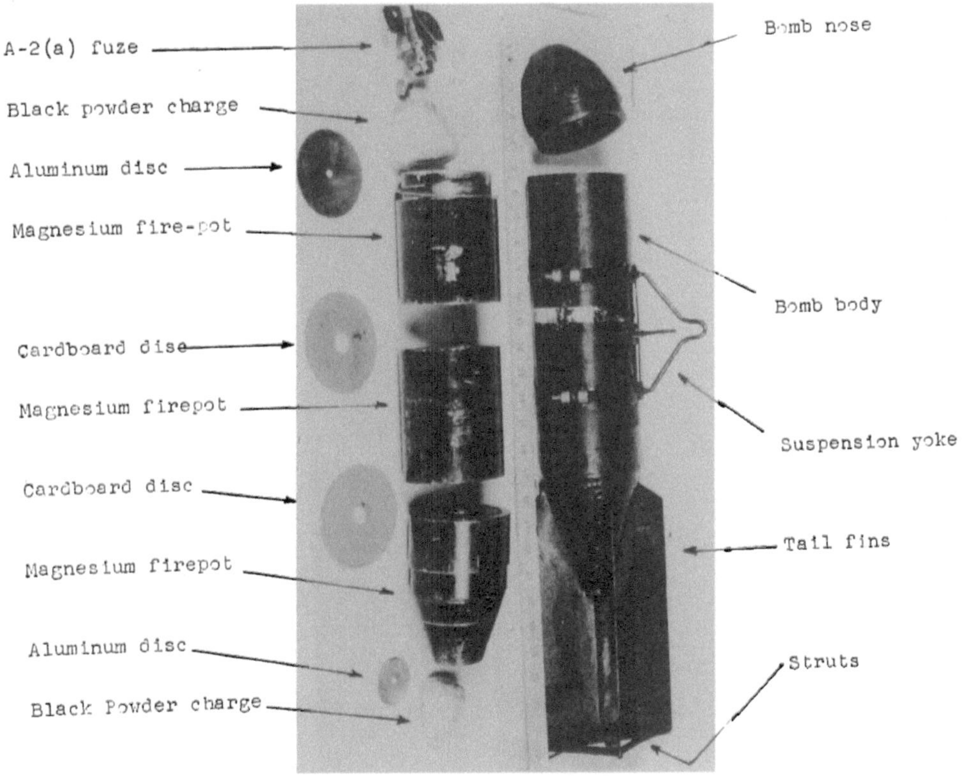

A-2(a) fuze

Black powder charge

Aluminum disc

Magnesium fire-pot

Cardboard disc

Magnesium firepot

Cardboard disc

Magnesium firepot

Aluminum disc

Black Powder charge

Bomb nose

Bomb body

Suspension yoke

Tail fins

Struts

Fig. 20

B - 4.5 kg. (candle type) incendiary bomb.
15 3/4 inches long and 3 3/4 inches in diameter.

Fig. 21

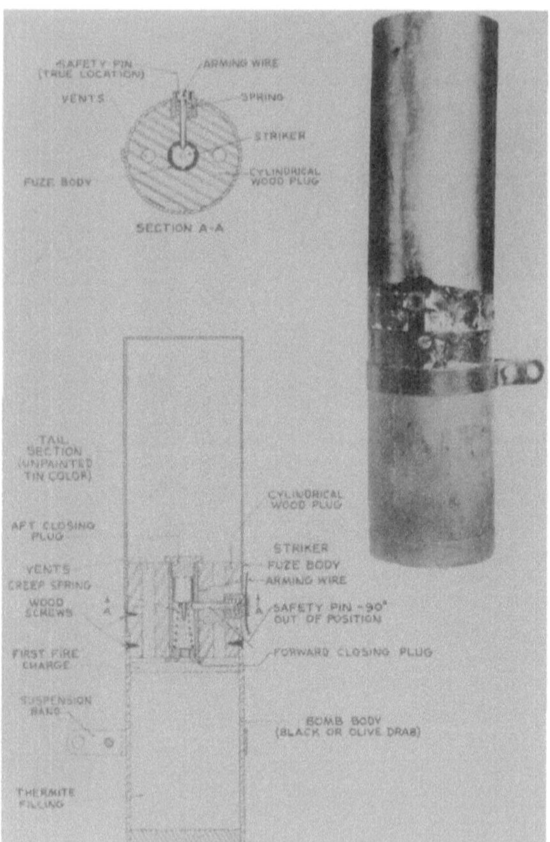

Fig. 22

<u>Column 34. Number of High explosive anti-personnel bombs</u>

<u>Column 35. Type high explosive anti-personnel bombs</u> Fig 23.

A - 15 kg. with A-2(b) fuze Type 92 Bomb

Fig. 23

Column 36. Numbers at the top of the envelope.

Miscelaneous pieces found
at Woodson, Texas
Figs. 22, 23, 24.

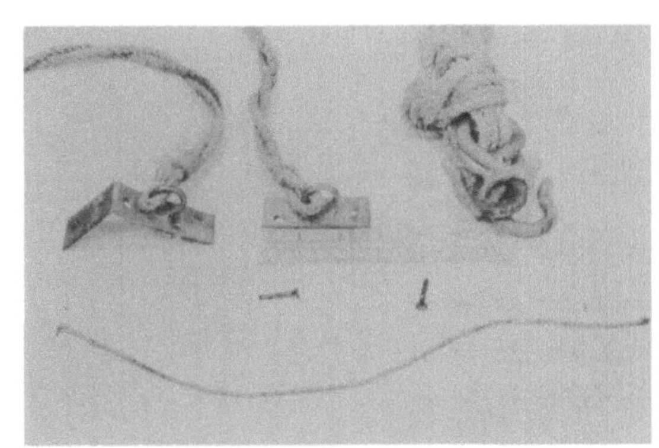

Fig. 22

Fig 23

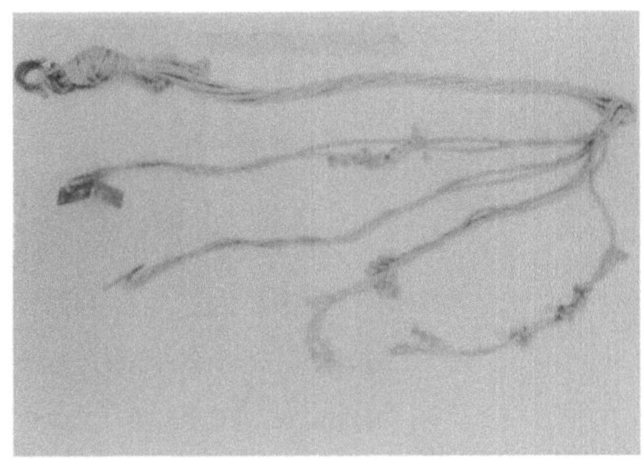

Fig. 24

ALASKA

No.	Date	Place	1 Envelope	2 No. Plies	3 Thickness	4 No. Gores	5 Width gores	6 Color	7 Env. Destructor	8 Type En.De.Fuse	9 Length of (8)	10 No. Shrouds	11 Type shrouds	12 Type valve	13 Valve marking	14 Valve number	15 Valve pressure	16 Shock absorber	17 Ballast gear	18 Battery	19 Ca Cl solution	20 Fr. Un. Plugs	21 Single Plugs	22 Type aneroid	23 Setting no. 1	24 Setting no. 2	25 Setting no. 3	26 Setting no. 4	27 Type bal. dest.	28 Wiring diagram	29 Arming wires	30 No. sandbags	31 Wt. sandbags	32 No. incendiary	33 Type "	34 No. H. E.	35 Type H. E.	36 No. top bag
1	23-12	Marshall	F					C		A		19	A	A		2569		0	A	A	10	14	1	A	12	15	9	—		B	3	2	5.5					
2	24-12	Holy Cross	F					B	A	A		19	A	B	W	1266		A	A		10	2								B		1	1.5					
3	5-1	Unalaska Aleutians	B																																			
4	24-1	Rat Island Aleutians	B																																			
5	25-1	Shimya	B																																			
6	8-2	Point Alexia Attu	B																																			
7	22-2	Ekwok Anchorage	✓											A						A																		
8	24-2	Attu 51-49N 172-06E	SO																																			
9	27-2	Bethel	SO										A																									
10	5-3	St. Lawrence Island	F																																			
11	7-3	Dillingham Nushagak bay	✓										A			1078																1E						
12	8-3	Platinum Good New Bay	✓																					A					A			3						
13	12-3	Nunapitchuk Bethel 2	F										A																									
14	13-3	Phillips	F																																			
15	15-3	Mumtrak Good News Bay	✓										A			8251																						
16	10-4	Midas Creek	F										A						A	A			1	•					A		4							
17	12-4	Massacre Bay Attu	SO																																			
18	13-4	Attu 9 balloons	SO																																			
19	14-4	Little Sitkin Island	D																																			
20	14-4	Amchitka	✓										A	B	W	1907		0	A					•														
21	28-4	Akiak 25M N. Bethel	✓											A	Y	10340							3								5	2						
22																																						
23																																						
24																																						
25																																						
26																																						
27																																						
28																																						
29																																						
30																																						
31																																						
32																																						
33																																						
34																																						

BRITISH COLUMBIA

NO.	DATE.	PLACE	1 Envelope	2 No. Plies	3 Thickness	4 No. Gores	5 Width gores	6 Color	7 Env. Destructor	8 Type En.De.Fuse	9 Length of (8)	10 No. Shrouds	11 Type shrouds	12 Type valve	13 Valve marking	14 Valve number	15 Valve pressure	16 Shock absorber	17 Ballast gear	18 Battery	19 Ca Cl solution	20 Pr. Un. Plugs	21 Single Plugs	22 Type aneroid	23 Setting no. 1	24 Setting no. 2	25 Setting no. 3	26 Setting no. 4	27 Type bal. dest.	28 Wiring diagram	29 Arming wires	30 No. sandbags	31 Wt. sandbags	32 No. incendiary	33 Type "	34 No. H. E.	35 Type H. E.	36 No. top bag
1	17-1	Boundary Bay	F																																			
2	19-2	Takla Landing	✓										A	B	W	9678		A	A	A		11		Δ					A			1						
3	22-2	Chase	F																																			
4	3-3	Duncan	✓																																			
5	3-3	Nanaimo	✓											A		8256			A															1				
6	5-3	Stuart Lake	F																																			
7	9-3	Nicola	✓																																	1	A	
8	10-3	Galiano Island	SD																																			
9	11-3	Kunghit Isl. Qu. Char.	SD																																			
10	12-3	Coal Harbor	✓											B		17520																		1	A			
11	12-3	Rupert Arm Inlet	✓																																			
12	13-3	Port Hardy	SD																												3							
13	14-3	Gambier Island	F																																			
14	17-3	Fort Babine	D											A		6274																						
15	18-3	Cedervale	✓											B		15031																		1				
16	20-3	Williams Lake	✓																A													5						
17	20-3	Denman Island	✓																A	A														2	B			
18	21-3	Ashcraft	✓																																			
19	22-3	Barriere	✓																																			
20	24-3	Jervis Inlet	F																																			
21	28-3	Whitewater Fort Ware	✓											B		5188																12		2	B			
22	31-3	Barrier Lake	✓										A																									
23	8-4	Merrit	✓										A	B	W	9878			A	A									A							1	A	
24	17-4	Boundary Bay	✓											B		13698																		1		1		
25	20-4	Vedder Mountain	✓																																			
26	20-4	Chilliwack	✓										A																									
27	24-4	Kitchener 49-08N 116-18W	✓										A																									
28	29-4	Dome Creek																																1	B			
29	29-4	Vanderhoof (STUART LAKE)	F																																			
30																																						
31																																						
32																																						
33																																						
34																																						

CALIFORNIA

No.	Date	Place	1 Envelope	2 No. Plies	3 Thickness	4 No. Gores	5 Width gores	6 Color	7 Env. Destructor	8 Type Ex.De.Fuse	9 Length of (8)	10 No. Shrouds	11 Type shrouds	12 Type valve	13 Valve marking	14 Valve number	15 Valve pressure	16 Shock absorber	17 Ballast gear	18 Battery	19 Ca Cl solution	20 Pr. Un. Plugs	21 Single Plugs	22 Type aneroid	23 Setting no. 1	24 Setting no. 2	25 Setting no. 3	26 Setting no. 4	27 Type bal. dest.	28 Wiring diagram	29 Arming wires	30 No. sandbags	31 Wt. sandbags	32 No. incendiary	33 Type "	34 No. H. E.	35 Type H. E.	36 No. top bag
1	4-11	San Pedro	R																																			
2	4-1	Sebastopol	F	5				B	A	A		19	A	A	S	4590		A	A					A	20	24	23	40mm	A	A	1			4E				
3	5-1	Napa	B																																			
4	10-1	Alturas	✓	5	A	60	20	B	A	A		19	A	B	W	3060		O	A	A											3							
5	15-1	Moorpark Ventura Saticoy	✓			54	11	C	A	A				B	W	5680						5														1E	A	
6	31-1	Julian	✓			38		A	A	A				B	W	11318		O	A	A					22	23	27	55mm	A	B	3							
7	1-2	Red Bluff	F					A						B	W	7100																						
8	1-2	Hayfork	✓										A	B	W	13821	.036	O	A	A		12		Δ	11.5	N 8	22	35mm	A	C	4	7	N	4	B			
9	8-2	Camp Beale Marysville	✓											B	W	13420		O				16	1						A		5							
10	12-2	Cohasset																																		1E	A	
11	21-2	Oxnard	✓																																			
12	23-2	Calistoga Elmira	F SD																																			
13	11-3	Meridian	F																																			
14	13-3	Grimes	F											B		13643						6	5									3		1 1	A B			
15	14-3	Big Bend Redding	✓										A	B	W	9052																						
16	18-3	Guerneville Cloverdale																																				
17	22-3	Volcano	✓			38							A	B		7363			A	A		6	8						A		1							
18																																						
19																																						
20																																						
21																																						
22																																						
23																																						
24																																						
25																																						
26																																						
27																																						
28																																						
29																																						
30																																						
31																																						
32																																						
33																																						
34																																						

No.	Date	Place	1 Envelope	2 No. Plies	3 Thickness	4 No. Gores	5 Width gores	6 Color	7 Env. Destructor	8 Type En.De.Fuse	9 Length of (8)	10 No. Shrouds	11 Type shrouds	12 Type valve	13 Valve marking	14 Valve number	15 Valve pressure	16 Shock absorber	17 Ballast gear	18 Battery	19 Ca Cl solution	20 Pr. Un. Plugs	21 Single Plugs	22 Type aneroid	23 Setting no. 1	24 Setting no. 2	25 Setting no. 3	26 Setting no. 4	27 Type bal. dest.	28 Wiring diagram	29 Arming wires	30 No. sandbags	31 Wt. sandbags	32 No. incendiary	33 Type	34 No. H. E.	35 Type H. E.	36 No. top bag
ALBERTA																																						
1	7-2	Provost	✓											B		11516			A	A									A									
2	22-2	Lethbridge Mannyberries	✓											A		4277			A				5	Δ					A									
3	10-3	Edson	✓																																			
4	11-3	Fort Chiewyan	✓											A		6376			A																			
5	13-3	Baril Lake	✓																																			
6	20-3	Delbourne	✓																															1	A			
7	20-3	Foremost	✓																																			
8	24-3	Medicine Hat	✓																																			
9	28-3	Strathmore	SP F										A	B		1508																						
10	29-3	Medicine Hat No. 2	✓																																			
11																																						
12																																						
13																																						
14																																						
15																																						
16																																						
17																																						
18																																						
19																																						
SASKATCHEWAN																																						
1	12-1	Minton																		A			A	A		26	23	13				4	55	2/1	B/A			
2	8-2	Moosejaw	✓										A	A		8236				A									A									
3	22-2	Saskatoon	✓										A	A	Y	8496			A																			
4	11-3	Camsell Portage	✓											A		4390			A	A														1	B			
5	14-3	Flinflon Marie Lake	✓										A																									
6	30-3	Consul																																1	A			
7	31-3	Ituna 51N 104W	✓											B		3345																						
8	1-4	Yorktown	✓																																			
9																																						
10																																						
11																																						
12																																						
13																																						
14																																						

No.	Date	Place	1 Envelope	2 No. Plies	3 Thickness	4 No. Gores	5 Width gores	6 Color	7 Env. Destructor	8 Type En.De.Fuse	9 Length of (8)	10 No. Shrouds	11 Type shrouds	12 Type valve	13 Valve marking	14 Valve number	15 Valve pressure	16 Shock absorber	17 Ballast gear	18 Battery	19 Ca Cl solution	20 Pr. Un. Plugs	21 Single Plugs	22 Type aneroid	23 Setting no. 1	24 Setting no. 2	25 Setting no. 3	26 Setting no. 4	27 Type bal. dest.	28 Wiring diagram	29 Arming wires	30 No. sandbags	31 Wt. sandbags	32 No. incendiary	33 Type "	34 No. H. E.	35 Type H. E.	36 No. top bag
		COLORADO																																				
4	13-3	Delta	F										A																									
2	20-3	Timnath																																1 IE	B A			
3																																						
4																																						
5																																						
		IDAHO																																				
1	8-2	Blackfoot	F					A																														
2	8-2	Twin falls	F																																			
3	11-2	American Falls	F										C																									
4	22-2	Rigby	✓			60			AE				A	A		8131		0	A	A									A		/							155
5	25-2	Boise	✓						A				A						A	A									A			/						
6	13-3	American Falls 2	F					C	A			19	A																									
7	22-3	Rogerson	✓										A	B		13548			A	A																		
8	24-4	Lucille	F																																			
9																																						
10																																						
11																																						
12																																						
13																																						
14																																						
15																																						
16																																						
17																																						
		Iowa																																				
1	2-2	Laurens	F					A	A			18	A	B	W	5751																						
2	13-3	Pocohantas	✓																																			
3																																						
4																																						
5																																						
		KANSAS																																				
1	23-2	Bigelow	✓	4					A	A	A	19	A	B		3347			A	A																		
2																																						
3																																						
4																																						

No.	Date	Place	1 Envelope	2 No. Plies	3 Thickness	4 No. Gores	5 Width gores	6 Color	7 Env. Destructor	8 Type En.De.Fuze	9 Length of (8)	10 No. Shrouds	11 Type shrouds	12 Type valve	13 Valve marking	14 Valve number	15 Valve pressure	16 Shock absorber	17 Ballast gear	18 Battery	19 Ca Cl solution	20 Pr. Un. Plugs	21 Single Plugs	22 Type aneroid	23 Setting no. 1	24 Setting no. 2	25 Setting no. 3	26 Setting no. 4	27 Type bal. dest.	28 Wiring diagram	29 Arming wires	30 No. sandbags	31 Wt. sandbags	32 No. incendiary	33 Typo "	34 No. H. E.	35 Type H. E.	36 No. top bag
		MANITOBA																																				
1	10-3	Nelson House																																IE	A			
2	12-3	Oxford House	✓										A	A		6629			A										O									
3	30-3	Waterhen Lake	✓																																			
4	10-4	Hudson Bay Post Indian L.	✓																																			
5	5-4	Lawford Lake	F																																			
6																																						
7																																						
8																																						
9																																						
10																																						
11																																						
12																																						
13																																						
		McKenzie																																				
1	19-1	Fort Simpson	✓					B	A	A				B		5596			A	A	10					26	23	–	A		3							
2	18-2	Marie River	F																																			
3																																						
4																																						
5																																						
		Michigan																																				
1	23-2	Grand Rapids	✓	4				C				19	A	A	S	6028			A	A																		
2																																						
3																																						
4																																						
		Nebraska																																				
1	2-2	Schuyler	F	5	A			A	A	A																												
2	12-2	Burwell	✓	5				B	D			19	A	A	G	6697			A	A		6		Δ						C	5			2	B			
3	19-3	Osceola	✓					A					B	W		13633																						
4	20-3	~~Burwell~~ CHADRON	✓						O			19	A	A		6161			A																			
5																																						
6																																						
7																																						
8																																						
9																																						

MISCELANEOUS

No.	Date	Place	1 Envelope	2 No. Plies	3 Thickness	4 No. Gores	5 Width gores	6 Color	7 Env. Destructor	8 Type En.De.Fuze	9 Length of (8)	10 No. Shrouds	11 Type shrouds	12 Type valve	13 Valve marking	14 Valve number	15 Valve pressure	16 Shock absorber	17 Ballast gear	18 Battery	19 Ca Cl solution	20 Pr. Un. Plugs	21 Single Plugs	22 Type aneroid	23 Setting no. 1	24 Setting no. 2	25 Setting no. 3	26 Setting no. 4	27 Type bal. dest.	28 Wiring diagram	29 Arming wires	30 No. sandbags	31 Wt. sandbags	32 No. incendiary	33 Type "	34 No. H. E.	35 Type H. E.	36 No. top bag
1	14-11	Kailua Hawaii	F	5	A			A					A					A	A	A					-	21	18	90mm	A	A	4							
2	12-1	San Eugenie Point	2 SD																																			
3	12-3	30-18N 132-52W	L											A	S	2919			A																			
4	12-3	700 M SW San Fransisco	✓																																			
5	18-3	Sonoyta Mexico	✓										A	B	W	17463																						
6	28-3	Laguna Salada Lake	SD																																			
7	15-4	52-46 N 178-30W	SD																																			
8	15-4	55-24N 172-24W	✓																																			
9	16-4	41-46N 171-47W	F																A																			
10	20-4	Watson Lake Yukon	F ✓																																			
11	20-4	Coahuila Mexico	✓																																			
12	23-4	120m Moresby Island	✓																																			
13	26-4	53-03N 135-52W	R			22									W	15																						
14																																						
15																																						
16																																						
17																																						
18																																						
19																																						
20																																						
21																																						
22																																						
23																																						
24																																						
25																																						
26																																						
27																																						
28																																						
29																																						
30																																						
31																																						
32																																						
33																																						
34																																						

		MONTANA	1 Envelope	2 No. Plies	3 Thickness	4 No. Gores	5 Width gores	6 Color	7 Env. Destructor	8 Type En.De.Fuze	9 Length of (8)	10 No. Shrouds	11 Type shrouds	12 Type valve	13 Valve marking	14 Valve number	15 Valve pressure	16 Shock absorber	17 Ballast gear	18 Battery	19 Ca Cl solution	20 Pr. Un. Plugs	21 Single Plugs	22 Type aneroid	23 Setting no. 1	24 Setting no. 2	25 Setting no. 3	26 Setting no. 4	27 Type bal. dest.	28 Wiring diagram	29 Arming wires	30 No. sandbags	31 Wt. sandbags	32 No. incendiary	33 " Type	34 No. H. E.	35 Type H. E.	36 No. top bag
1	15-11	Kalispell	✓	5	A	60	21	C	A	A		19	A	B	W	1241	.06	A																				
2	12-1	Lame Deer	✓			38	32	A	A	A		19	A	A		2621																						
3	9-2	Lodgegrass	✓			60		A																														
4	12-2	Hardin	F									19	A	B	W	9036																		1E	A			
5	12-2	Riverdale																																3E	B			
6	12-2	Eden	F	5		60		B	O	O		19	A																									
7	17-2	Polson-Flathead Lake	B F	5				B																														
8	22-2	Hays	✓			60		A	O			19	A	A	Y	8220		O	A													3						133
9	23-2	Boyd	✓					A				19	A						A	A									A		4	1						
10	25-2	Laurel	✓										A																									
11	10-3	Whitehall	✓			60	19	A	O	O		19	A	A	S W	2391 1104		O	A	A	10	O	O						A		1	1		2	B			
12	10-3	Harlowton																													3	3		1E	A			
13	10-3	Bernice	✓			60		C					A						A																			
14	12-3	Sula																																1E				
15	13-3	Divide	✓			60	19	A	O	O				B	W	15944		O	A	A		?	29								2							
16	13-3	Benchland	✓									19	A						A												2							
17	13-3	Legg	✓			60						17	A			15698			A			18																
18	13-3	Broadus-Hammond	1/3									17	A																									
19	16-3	Nyak- coram	F																																			
20	18-3	Glen-Reichle																																1	B			
21	30-3	Bozeman	✓					A					A			NONE			A	A												4E						
22	6-4	Turner	✓																																			
23	21-4	Phillipsburg	✓											B	W	1799																						
24	25-4	Loring-Dodsnn	F										A																									
25																																						
26																																						
27																																						
28																																						
29																																						
30																																						
31																																						
32																																						
33																																						
34																																						

No.	Date	Place	1 Envelope	2 No. Plies	3 Thickness	4 No. Gores	5 Width gores	6 Color	7 Env. Destructor	8 Type En.De.Fuse	9 Length of (8)	10 No. Shrouds	11 Type shrouds	12 Type valve	13 Valve marking	14 Valve number	15 Valve pressure	16 Shock absorber	17 Ballast gear	18 Battery	19 Ca Cl solution	20 Pr. Un. Plugs	21 Single Plugs	22 Type aneroid	23 Setting no. 1	24 Setting no. 2	25 Setting no. 3	26 Setting no. 4	27 Type bal. dest.	28 Wiring diagram	29 Arming wires	30 No. sandbags	31 Wt. sandbags	32 No. incendiary	33 Type	34 No. H. E.	35 Type H. E.	36 No. top bag
		NEVADA																																				
1	9-11	Yerington	R																D	D																		
2	22-3	Reno	B SD					C				19	A						A	A		12	3	Δ								1		2	B			
3	29-3	Pyrmid Lake Nixon	✓			36		C	O	O			A	B	W	7948			A			11	1	Δ							5	4						
4	8-4	Vya Massacre Lake	✓										A	A	S	2590			A												5							
5	22-4	Elko	F											B	W	13934																						
6																																						
7																																						
8																																						
9																																						
10																																						
		North Dakota																																				
1	22-2	Ashley	✓					A				19	A	A	S	6346																						
2	30-[illegible]	Grafton	✓					C					A	B		19651			A	A				Δ					A			?						
3																																						
4																																						
5																																						
		South Dakota																																				
1	12-2	Nowlin Rapid City																														1		2E	B			
2	25-2	Ree Heights Wolsey	✓					A											A	A			1	•					A									
3	30-3	Red Elm	✓			38							A	B	W	15663			A	A				•														
4	31-3	Marcus																																1E	A			
5	26-4	Buffalo	F																																			
6																																						
7																																						
8																																						
9																																						
10																																						
		Texas																																				
1	24-3	Desdemona	F			40	30	A	A	A		19	A	B	W	1366		O	A	A														2E	A			
2	24-3	Woodson	✓					B	O			19	A																									
3																																						
4																																						
5																																						

No.	Date	ORBGON Place	1 Envelope	2 No. Plies	3 Thickness	4 No. Gores	5 Width gores	6 Color	7 Env. Destructor	8 Type En.De.Fuse	9 Length of (8)	10 No. Shrouds	11 Type shrouds	12 Type valve	13 Valve marking	14 Valve number	15 Valve pressure	16 Shock absorber	17 Ballast gear	18 Battery	19 Ca Cl solution	20 Pr. Un. Plugs	21 Single Plugs	22 Type aneroid	23 Setting no. 1	24 Setting no. 2	25 Setting no. 3	26 Setting no. 4	27 Type bal. dest.	28 Wiring diagram	29 Arming wires	30 No. sandbags	31 Wt. sandbags	32 No. incendiary	33 Type	34 No. H. E.	35 Type H. E.	36 No. top bag
1	31-12	Estacada	✓			64	23	A	A	A				A	S	2647		A	F	A																		
2	4-1	Medford																																1E	B			
3	2-2	Ontario Vale	F	4				A				19	A						F																			
4	22-2	Northbend	SD			60		C	A	A		19	A																					?				
5	23-2	Burns	✓			44		C						B	W	3841			A	A												1						
6	26-2	Eugene	✓											A	W	10337																						
7	23-2	Deer Island	F																																			
8	10-3	Wolf Creek	F					C																														
9	13-3	Pendleton Echo	✓			60			A	A			A	B		15941			A	A		22	1						A		3	11	8/4	1	B			
10	13-3	Coquille Riverton	F																																			
11	13-3	Malheur Lake	✓						A	A			A						A															1	B			
12	17-3	Yamhill	F																															1				
13	20-3	The Dalles																																1E	B			
14	21-3	Murphy	F																																			
15	22-3	Rome	✓						O	O			A	A	Y	10305			A	A									A		3							
16	23-3	Parkersburg	✓																																			
17	29-3	Mitchell Butte Nyssa																														2				1	A	
18	14-4	Grants Pass	F																																			
19	23-4	Lake of the Woods	F										A					A	A										A									
20	26-4	Beatty	F																																			
21	2-5	Huntington	F																																			
22	5-5	Bly	✓						A					B	W	5893													A			8		4	B	1E	A	
23																																						
24																																						
25																																						
26																																						
27																																						
28																																						
29																																						
30																																						
31																																						
32																																						
33																																						
34																																						

No.	Date	Place	1 Envelope	2 No. Plies	3 Thickness	4 No. Gores	5 Width gores	6 Color	7 Env. Destructor	8 Type Hn.De.Fuse	9 Length of (8)	10 No. Shrouds	11 Type shrouds	12 Type valve	13 Valve marking	14 Valve number	15 Valve pressure	16 Shock absorber	17 Ballast gear	18 Battery	19 Ca Cl solution	20 Pr. Un. Plugs	21 Single Plugs	22 Type aneroid	23 Setting no. 1	24 Setting no. 2	25 Setting no. 3	26 Setting no. 4	27 Type bal. dest.	28 Wiring diagram	29 Arming wires	30 No. sandbags	31 Wt. sandbags	32 No. incendiary	33 Type "	34 No. H. E.	35 Type H. E.	36 No. top bag
		UTAH																																				
1	23-2	Tremonton	✓					C	A	A	0	19	A	B	W	3447		0	A	A	18			Δ	6.3	Δ3.2	23	34mm	A	C	5							
2	18-3	Garrison	✓					A			0	19	A	A	Y	1049#			A	A		28										5						
3	30-3	Duschesne	✓						0	0	0	19	A	B	W	1999		0	A	A				Δ					A									
4	16-4	Snowville	F																																			
5	25-4	Paragona	F																																			
6																																						
7																																						
8																																						
9																																						
10																																						
11																																						
		WYOMING																																				
1	6-12	Thermopolis	F																																	1E	A	
2	19-1	Manderson	F					A																														
3	28-1	Worland	✓										A			308																						
4	8-2	Newcastle	✓					B				19	A	B	W	9060		0	A																			
5	9-2	Casper	F																																			
6	22-2	Powell	F	4				A					1	B	W	3468			A	A														2 1	B A			
7	22-2	Glendo	✓			60			0			19	A	A	S	4895			A					Δ							2	2	6	1	B			124
8	22-2	Kirby	✓			60								B		2354		0	A	A				Δ	10	Δ9.7	16.7	42mm	A	C	5	1						
9	22-3	Basin Sheridan	F																																			
10	21-3	Gillette	F																																			
11	6-4	Casper 2	✓																																			
12																																						
13																																						
14																																						
15																																						
16																																						
17																																						
18																																						
19																																						
20																																						
21																																						
22																																						

WASHINGTON

No.	Date	Place	1 Envelope	2 No. Plies	3 Thickness	4 No. Gores	5 Width gores	6 Color	7 Env. Destructor	8 Type En.De.Fuze	9 Length of (8)	10 No. Shrouds	11 Type shrouds	12 Type valve	13 Valve marking	14 Valve number	15 Valve pressure	16 Shock absorber	17 Ballast gear	18 Battery
1	12-2	Spokane																		
2	14-2	Prosser	✓											A		6997		0	A	A
3	21-2	Sumas	SD																	
4	21-2	Ephrata																		
5	25-2	Goldendale	F D										A	A		8478				
6	28-2	Tacoma	F																	
7	4-3	Puyallup Orting	F					C												
8	10-3	Toppenish	B					A						B		3378				
9	10-3	Ephrata number 2	SD ✓					A				19	A	B		3398			A	A
10	10-3	Satus Pass	✓			38								A		12051			A	A
11	10-3	Moxee	✓													NONE				
12	11-3	Cold Creek	SD			60			A	A				A		6767			A	A
13	13-3	Everrett Paine Field	✓																	
14	13-3	Chimacum Port Townsend	SD																	
15	13-3	Farmington	✓			60			A	A		19	A			13729			A	
16	1-4	Colville	✓						A				A							
17	5-4	Walla Walla	✓										A	B	W	17181			A	A
18	3-5	Mount Ranier	B																	
19																				
20																				
21																				
22																				
23																				
24																				
25																				
26																				
27																				
28																				
29																				
30																				
31																				
32																				
33																				
34																				

No.	19 Ca Cl solution	20 Pr. Un. Plugs	21 Single Plugs	22 Type aneroid	23 Setting no. 1	24 Setting no. 2	25 Setting no. 3	26 Setting no. 4	27 Type bal. dest.	28 Wiring diagram	29 Arming wires	30 No. sandbags	31 Wt. sandbags	32 No. incendiary	33 Type "	34 No. H. E.	35 Type H. E.	36 No. top bag
1														1 1	A B			
2				Δ	2.6	Δ63	22	36mm			5							
3																		
4												3						
5																		
6																		
7																		
8		15	1								4	1		3E	B			
9		23										3		4	B			
10		13	3								3	1						
11				2					A					2	B			
12											3	7						
13														1	B			
14																		
15									A									
16																		
17			4						A		1							
18																		
19																		
20																		
21																		
22																		
23																		
24																		
25																		
26																		
27																		
28																		
29																		
30																		
31																		
32																		
33																		
34																		

NAVAL RESEARCH LABORATORY

C-455-HAT
Anacostia Station

C-455-5/45
as
Washington 20, D. C.

8 January 1945

To: Officer in Charge
Technical Air Intelligence Center
U. S. Naval Air Station
Anacostia, D.C.

Subj: Kalispell Paper Balloon

Ref: (a) Visit of Lt.(jg) C. L. Miller of Technical Air Intelligence Center, USNAS, Anacostia to NRL on 26 Dec 1944.

1. At the request of the Technical Air Intelligence Center (reference (a)), the Laboratory has made a study of the subject balloon. Personnel of the Chemistry and Radio Divisions of the Laboratory and from the Lighter than Air Design Section of the Bureau of Aeronautics have conducted an investigation and their findings are presented herewith. No positive conclusion has been reached as to the place of origin and purpose of the balloon but it is believed either to have been sent up in the eastern Pacific area to obtain weather information or in Japan as an anti-aircraft device or to obtain weather information. The investigation is being continued and any further information of importance will be forwarded.

DISCOVERY

2. This balloon was discovered in the snow near Kalispell, Montana on 11 December 1944. The amount of snow on the balloon when discovered indicated that it had landed between 11 November and 25 November 1944. After inspection at the discovery site by F.B.I. and Army and Navy representatives, the material was forwarded to Technical Air Intelligence Center, NAS, Anacostia and from there it was brought to the Naval Research Laboratory for examination.

INVENTORY

3. The material received at NRL for examination consisted of the balloon envelope, the shrouds, a relief valve, a length of fuze, an ignition or flash charge and a rubber-rope assembly probably intended to act as a shock absorber. Two containers of melted snow from the discovery area were also received.

PAPER ENVELOPE

4. The envelope was a true sphere 100 feet in circumference and weighing 152 pounds. Assuming the balloon is filled to capacity with hydrogen the net lifting power (buoyance less weight of envelope) at various altitudes is as follows:

Altitude	Lifting Power
Sea level	1033 pounds
0.9 miles	876 "
5.0 "	360 "
6.8 "	210 "

5. The envelope has a circular opening at the base where the valve was attached when discovered. There is a skirt for attachment of the shrouds located below the equator of the balloon. The ignition charge was attached to

the envelope between the skirt and the equator. At the top of the envelope was a circular patch ruled off and bearing printed and written Japanese characters. The translation of these characters reveal that the patch is a record of manufacturing data showing in part that this balloon was a type No. 2, best quality, inspected 10 October 1944 and completed 31 October 1944.

6. The material of the envelope consists of 5 layers of thin long fiber paper cemented together with hydrocellulose, a parchmentized form of cellulose. The long fiber paper gives high strength and the hydrocellulose gives gas impermeability. The degradation of the cellulose to hydrocellulose has been carried so far that 20% of the total weight of the balloon material is water soluble. The material increases 67% in weight when wet.

7. The tensile strength of the material dry is 68 pounds per linear inch and wet is 37 pounds per inch. The thickness ranges from .0075 to .009 inch. The balloon inflated to 1 oz. per square inch pressure would be under a skin tension of six pounds per linear inch. A 1000 pound weight hanging from the shroud lines would add an additional pound per linear inch tension along the junction of the skirt with the envelope. The balloon is therefor amply strong to withstand an internal pressure of 1 oz. per square inch plus a load of 1000 lbs.

8. The hydrogen permeability of the envelope material is 0.98 liters per square meter per 24 hours. This is about one-tenth the permeability of ordinary rubberized balloon fabric. The rate of loss for the balloon would roughly be 10 cu. ft. every 24 hours so there would be no significant decrease in lifting power due to diffusion in a week. The hydrogen permeability was determined on a 68 square inch sample with hydrogen at one atmosphere on one side and air at one atmosphere on the other. The air was drawn past the membrane and its hydrogen content determined by analysis. A repetition of the experiment using 1 oz. excess pressure on the hydrogen side gave the same permeability.

9. A sample of the envelope material has been sent to an expert on Japanese papers for further examination.

VALVE ASSEMBLY

10. The valve seat is pressed .041 inch sheet steel and consists of a 19.5 inch diameter cylindrical section which was cemented into the paper envelope. Below the cylindrical section the seat flanges inward and then down to form a second cylindrical section 16 inches in diameter and 1 inch high. The external end of the lower cylindrical section is upset to form a round contact surface upon which the valve seats. The valve is a pressed steel disc 17 inches in diameter and is forced against the valve seat by a compressed coil spring under adjustable tension. The coil spring is guided by an axial bolt through the valve sliding into a sleeve which is supported on three steel arms extending to the flange section of the valve seat where they are bolted fast. The adjustable spring tension was set to release gas from the balloon when the pressure reached a valve of 0.06 pounds (1 ounce) per square inch. A 7/64 inch hole had been drilled through the valve near the edge.

11. Six small rope loops are fastened to the upper cylindrical section of the valve seat and on each of these loops there is two short lengths of rope with cut ends. Possibly the balloon was attached to the filling tube by these ropes. The valve and valve spring assembly may have been bolted on to the seat after filling the balloon.

C-455-HAT
C-455-5/45
as

12. The valve parts apparently have been made by mass production methods using forming dies made purposely for this job. The number "1241" is painted on the valve.

13. A fragment of a paper tag was attached to one of the rope loops on the valve seat. In a column adjacent to the torn edge the numbers "18, 19, 20 and 21" were written in ink.

SHROUDS

14. The shroud lines are 1 inch in circumference 3 strand manila ropes 45 feet long. There are 19 such lines gathered together at the lower end and knotted to a small triangular steel ring. Each line branches by splicing into two lines about five feet from the upper end. There is a steel hook at each upper end for joining to the skirt of the balloon envelope. The shroud lines are strong enough to support several times the maximum lifting power of the balloon.

FUZE

15. The fuze was a paper cord type with a slow burning core. The burning rate was 66 seconds per foot and the length was reported to be 62 feet when discovered, which would give a burning time of slightly over one hour. The free end of the fuze apparently was cut off and lost at Kalispell. There is conflicting testimony as to whether or not the fuze had been lit. The free end received at NRL refused to ignite and it was necessary to ignite a freshly cut end. Possibly there was a small dead section at the free end. The fuze would be difficult to ignite electrically. A sample of core filling material, on being lighted, burned fitfully and went out before all of the material was consumed.

IGNITION CHARGE

16. The ignition charge consisted of a paper container about the size and shape of a narrow mouth 6 oz. glass bottle. This contained 250 grams of magnesium flash powder. The base of the container was cemented to the balloon envelope and the fuze was tied in through the outer end. The magnesium charge would be ignited by the fuze to produce a flash explosion capable of rupturing and igniting the balloon. The flash would be similar to that obtained with photographic flash powder.

RUBBER-ROPE SHOCK ABSORBER

17. The rubber portion of this assembly consisted of 3/64 inch square strands of soft rubber similar to our pre-war rubber bands. About 250 strands were gathered together at the ends and covered with a woven cotton cover. The covered portions were looped back and siezed with heavy cord to form eyes. The net result is a rubber cable 22 inches long having cotton covered eyes at either end and an uncovered rubber midsection between the eyes 10 inches long. Eight strands of 1-1/8 inch circumference manila rope have been knotted to both eyes to form a sister which limits the amount of elongation of the rubber shock absorber. At one eye the sister forms a loop carrying two open steel hooks facing in opposite directions. The other eye is abraded and discolored and the rope knot at this eye is also abraded and discolored. The indication is that the two metal hooks were hooked into the shroud line ring and that some sort of metal hook fastened into the eye on the other, or lower, end of the shock abosrber. The free rope ends at either end of the shock absorber are badly frayed and discolored. It appears probable, but not certain, that the only weight the balloon carried was hooked to the lower eye of the

shock absorber. The shape of the knot at the upper end and the location of the worn area of the rope around the hooks indicates that the weight was carried by the rubber rather than the rope.

18. The frayed and discolored condition of all rope ends discourages the idea that any additional weight could have been carried on the rope directly and cut loose. The rope ends are too short to have been knotted to anything. The size of the shroud ring suggests that only one such shock absorber was intended to be hooked on.

19. The shock absorber assembly was stretched under measured loads using the hooks at the upper end and the lower eye as points of connection. The results were as follows:

Load	Rubber	Rope Sister	Estimated percent of load on: Rubber	Rope
20 lbs.	Taut	Slack	100%	0%
50 "	"	"	100	0
75 "	"	Tightening	80	20
100 "	"	Taut	60	40
125 "	"	"	50	50
150 "	"	"	40	60
200 "	"	"	25	75
225 "	"	"	20	80

The load was then released measuring the overall length.

Load	Length
225 lbs.	42-1/4 inches
200 "	42 "
175 "	41-3/4 "
150 "	41-1/2 "
125 "	41 "
100 "	40-1/2 "
75 "	39 "
50 "	35 "
25 "	31-1/2 "
5 "	29-1/2 "
0 "	28-1/2 "

20. These results indicate that the shock absorber would not be very efficient for a load in excess of 100 pounds and ineffective for a load exceeding 150 pounds. At 150 pounds the siezed eyes on the rubber begin to slip exposing a clean surface of the cotton covering. At 200 pounds the slippage is pronounced and failure would result after a short period due to the tendency of the rubber to creep out of the siezing. It seems probable that the shock absorber was intended for a load not exceeding 100 pounds and that it has never been used with a load exceeding 150 pounds.

MELTED SNOW FROM DISCOVERY AREA

21. One of the two containers of melted snow was opened at the Laboratory and found to contain about 25 cc's of water. The water contained tiny fragments of paper and was weakly basic in reaction. Treating clean water briefly with the balloon envelope material, produced identical results. There was no evidence of any chemical material in the melted snow other than what would result from contact with the balloon envelope.

C-455-HAT
C-455-5/45
as

22. The reports from Kalispell mention the finding of a "frozen residue" or "yellow solid" having a tear gas odor and slightly irritating to the skin and eyes. No evidence of any such material has been observed at the Laboratory. If the balloon were filled with hydrogen generated by chemical means and not purified, various impurities in the gas might form such a residue.

GAS USED IN THE BALLOON

23. In all probability the balloon was filled with hydrogen since this would be the cheapest and most efficient. A second possibility is the use of water gas, a mixture of hydrogen and carbon monoxide formed by passing steam over hot coke. The use of this mixture would reduce the lifting power to less than 1/7 the values given for hydrogen. Methane could also be used and this would also give a lifting power less than 1/7 that of hydrogen. Ammonia would be expensive, give low lifting power and probably have a detectable odor.

RADAR DETECTION

24. In the opinion of several radar experts, the balloon envelope would not be radar-visible. The steel relief valve would be visible but due to the small size it would probably pass unnoticed through a radar searched zone. The chances of detection at 10,000 feet would be small and at higher altitudes negligible. These conclusions will be checked by sending aloft a facsimile of the valve.

SOURCE AND PURPOSE

25. While the balloon is undoubtedly of Japanese manufacture, the evidence this far available does not permit any definite conclusion as to how and why it arrived at Kalispell. The large size of the balloon indicates that it was intended either to carry a heavy load or to attain an extremely high altitude, perhaps 50,000 feet, or to carry a moderate load at 30,000 or 40,000 feet. The shock absorber suggests that the load lifted was not large and that the objective was to attain considerable altitude. The fuze and ignition charge are intended to destroy the balloon after from one to a few hours, either to avoid detection or possibly to recover equipment sent aloft or to avoid interference with subsequent operations of a similar nature. Since the balloon was fuzed for self-destruction after a short time, it is unlikely that it was equipped with automatic ballast release equipment. Without ballast release the chances of the balloon remaining aloft more than 24 hours are small but do exist. With 1 ounce excess pressure in the balloon it could exceed its equilibrium ceiling by not more than 300 feet and it could withstand a temperature drop at constant barometric pressure of not more than 4-1/2°C. Under very favorable conditions, the balloon might remain within these limits until gas leakage reduced the internal pressure appreciably. If the balloon reaches even momentarily a condition in which the internal pressure is equal to external pressure and the buoyancy equals or is less than the load, then the balloon will fall to earth. Meteorological records are being investigated to determine whether favorable conditions for long continued flight prevailed at any time during the period in which the balloon may have been aloft.

26. At altitudes above around 20,000 feet the balloon would be carried in an easterly direction at a speed of 30 to 60 miles per hour, perhaps even faster. At 25,000 feet there is reputed to be a 60 mile per hour air current which crosses Japan, veers southward to Hawaii, then swings to the north crossing Northern California and on over Montana, where it again veers southward. This current was mapped by Von Bemmeln from cirrus cloud movements and is reproduced in several meteorological texts. Similar air currents were

C-455-HAT
C-455-5/45
as

observed at 20,000 to 40,000 feet over South Dakota by Major Stevens in his stratosphere balloon flights in 1934 and 1935. Similar balloons have been photographed over Japan but there is no proof that they are identical with the Kalispell balloon.

27. The balloon may therefor, by a sequence of events, namely; failure of the fuze, loss of load carried and favorable weather conditions, have come all the way from Japan. On the other hand it may have been released in the eastern Pacific from a submarine or otherwise. The shipping space for the balloon and shrouds would not exceed 25 cubic feet. Inflation for a load of 100 pounds would require less than 5,000 cubic feet of hydrogen. This would require 20 cylinders of 250 cubic feet capacity, or 2-1/2 cubic feet of calcium hydride, or 2-1/4 cubic feet of lithium hydride. The use of lithium or calcium hydride would require some gas generating apparatus. The inflation of a balloon from a submarine would be difficult but not impossible.

28. In the following table are tabulated the various suggested theories as to origin and purpose of the balloon, with arguments pro and con.

Source	Purpose	Pro	Con
Eastern Pacific	Radiosonde	1) Useful information not otherwise obtainable. 2) Fuzed to prevent detection of this activity. 3) Maximum load within capacity of shock absorber. 4) High altitude would explain large size of balloon.	
Eastern Pacific	Incendiary		1) Need for fuze not apparent unless balloon was released close in and destined for coastal area. 2) Not effective at this season.
Eastern Pacific	Bomb	1) Of some value as a propaganda and morale weapon. 2) Fuzed to regulate distance and assure fast descent.	1) Practically useless from a military standpoint. 2) Use would lead to search for and probable destruction of launching submarine.
Eastern Pacific	Personnel	1) Fuzed to destroy evidence after landing.	1) Balloon is larger than necessary for this use at maximum altitude for human survival without elaborate equipment.

C-455-HAT
C-455-5/45
as

Source	Purpose	Pro	Con
			2) Could devise simpler methods to accomplish same objective.
Eastern Pacific	Insect Pests or disease germs.	1) A morale weapon	1) Of doubtful effectiveness. 2) Smaller balloons could be used.
Japan	Plane Detection.	1) Fuzed to recover equipment	1) Photos over Japan show at least 13 balloons in a small area at one time. One or two would be sufficient.
Japan	Plane interference through dangling cable or other device.	1) Plausible means of air raid protection. 2) Would explain why several would be in air at one time. 3) Fuzed to recover equipment before balloon drifted too far or to clear air after raid.	
Japan	Radiosonde	1) Fuzed to recover equipment	1) Would not send up

29. From the above tabulation and the preceding discussion it appears that the balloon was probably not used to transport personnel. It was used either as a means of getting equipment into the air or of carrying some object into this country. The equipment or object could easily become detached accidentally. For one thing, the balloon may have descended once, scraped along the ground until the equipment fell off, and then reascended and traveled farther because of the decreased load.

30. The most plausible theories as to the source and use of the balloon in order of decreasing probability according to present evidence are:

1 - Released in eastern Pacific to obtain weather information, possibly a part of a world wide weather espionage system.
2 - Released in Japan as air raid protection through dangling cable or similar means.
3 - Released in Japan to obtain weather information.
4 - Released in eastern Pacific, possibly just as an experiment or propaganda gesture, to carry some object into this country.

31. In connection with theory No. 4 the wholesale introduction of incendiaries into the western forest areas during the dry season might be of some military importance.

NAVY DEPARTMENT
BUREAU OF AERONAUTICS
Washington 25, D.C.

Aer-E-191-CPB

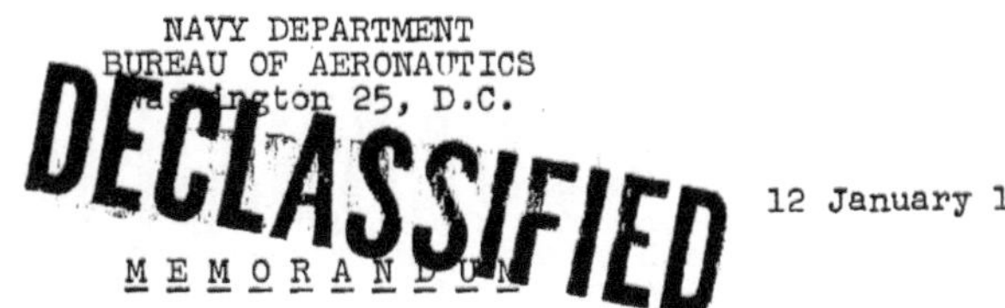

12 January 1945

M E M O R A N D U M

From: LTA Design Branch.
To: Op-16-V-T, Room 1W32.

Subj: Japanese Balloons.

Refs: (a) Conf. Memo C-455-HAT, C-455-5/45, dated 8 Jan. 1945.
(b) Conf. Memo C-455-HAT, C-455-6/45, dated 9 Jan. 1945.

1. This branch concurs in the discussion in ref. (a) on the "Kalispell Paper Balloon" with the following exceptions:

(a) Gas Used. It is considered most probable that the balloon was inflated with hydrogen, but methane or a half-and-half mixture of carbon monoxide and hydrogen have nearly half the gross lift of hydrogen instead of only one-seventh as stated in ref. (a). Taking the molecular weights of air, hydrogen, and methane as 29, 2, and 16, respectively, and the unit weight of air as 0.0765 lb./ft.^{3} at sea level, the unit lifts are 0.0765 x (29-2)/29 = 0.0712 lb./ft.^{3} for pure hydrogen, and 0.0765 x (29-16)/29 = 0.0343 lb./ft.^{3} for methane. A half-and-half mixture of carbon monoxide and hydrogen has slightly greater lift than methane, and ammonia a little less.

(b) Source and Purpose. The opinion is expressed in ref. (a) that it is not considered that the balloon was equipped with an automatic ballasting device. This branch does not concur because it is considered that without such a device the balloon could not have remained in the air more than a few hours. Only 1% difference between weight and buoyancy would cause a vertical velocity of about 400 ft./min. Moreover, it is understood that paper balloons found subsequently to the Kalispell balloon carried a device which appears to have been intended to drop loads, but because of the elaborate nature of the device, this branch is of the opinion that these loads were not merely ballast. It is suggested that they were anti-electronic devices, possibly with small explosive charges for opening the packages.

2. With a ballasting device and very favorable weather conditions, including a stable atmosphere and absence of sunlight, it is believed that the balloon could go through several cycles of up and down motion, and possibly remain in the air as long as three days. The distance it might drift in that time is a problem for the aerologists.

3. As conjectured in ref. (a), the balloon may have been intended for any condition between a heavy load at low altitude to a light load at 40,000 ft. or more. Perhaps it was intended to begin its flight with a heavy load and gain altitude as the load was dropped by the automatic device.

4. The rubberized silk balloon recovered from the ocean near San Pedro and described in ref. (b) is a very interesting example of a high-pressure constant-volume balloon which would be very stable, and with an automatic ballasting device might have stayed in the air for several weeks in favorable weather conditions. It was most probably intended for aerological purposes.

Aer-E-191-CPB

5. This branch concurs with the analysis in ref. ([illegible]) with the exception of the statement in paragraph 29 that the balloon could descend one mile from an altitude of four miles without loss of equilibrium. Even if the balloon were at its maximum super-pressure of 1 lb./in.^{2} at 4 miles altitude, a descent of 0.66 mile would wipe out the super-pressure, except in so far as the elastic contraction of the balloon with loss of pressure causes retention of the super-pressure, but since the balloon appears to have been fully stretched and to have very little residual elasticity, this would not affect conditions appreciably. If the balloon descended below the level of no super-pressure, it would continue down unless checked by dropping ballast or the occurrence of superheat.

C. P. Burgess.

NAVAL RESEARCH LABORATORY

Anacostia Station

Washington 20, D. C.

C-EF37(455-LBL)

C-455-7/45
as

CONFIDENTIAL

15 January 1945

To: Officer in Charge
Technical Air Intelligence Center
U. S. Naval Air Station
Anacostia, D. C.

Subj: Estacado Paper Balloon - CEE No. 22164

Refs: (a) Visit of Lt.(jg) C. L. Miller of TAIS, USNAS, Anacostia to NRL on 10 Jan 1945.
(b) NRL ltr C-455-HAT C-455-5/45as of 8 Jan 1945 to OinC, TAIC, USNAS, Anacostia in regard to the Kalispell Paper Balloon.

Encls: (HW)
(A) Photograph - View of Envelope
(B) Photograph - View of Relief Valve

1. At the request of the Technical Air Intelligence Center (reference (a)), the Laboratory has made a study of the balloon found at Estacado, Oregon. The balloon envelope and such appurtenances as were found indicate that the Kalispell balloon and the Estacado balloon were identical in design and probably identical in purpose. Not enough additional information has been found to warrant changing the conclusions already made as to the possible origin and purpose of these balloons.

DISCOVERY

2. The balloon was found hanging in a tree near Estacado, Oregon on 31 December 1944. It was believed to have been in the tree three or four days. After preliminary examination it was forwarded to Technical Air Intelligence Center, Naval Air Station, Anacostia and from there brought to NRL for examination. It was received at NRL on 10 January 1945.

INVENTORY

3. The material received at NRL for examination consisted of the balloon envelope and relief valve, the shroud lines, a fuze and ignition charge for destruction of the balloon, two other lengths of fuze, sections of rope and a rubber shock-absorber connecting the shroud lines to the remains of a metal framework, several rubber-insulated wires and two small segments of a bakelite ring containing a number of electrical contacts connected in pairs.

PAPER ENVELOPE

4. The envelope is a sphere 100 feet in circumference and is similar in design and lifting power to the Kalispell paper balloon, described in reference (b). There is no Japanese writing on the envelope. There are traces of a waxy flammable coating on the outer surface of the paper - probably to decrease water absorption by the paper. A photograph of the uninflated balloon is shown in enclosure (A).

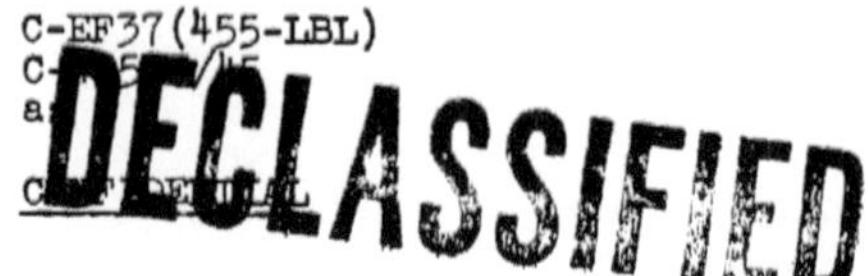

VALVE ASSEMBLY

5. The valve assembly consists of a cylindrical section 19-½" in diameter and a valve 17" in diameter. A coil spring of adjustable tension holds the valve face against the seat where a seal is made with a thin rubber gasket. The assembly is similar to that of the Kalispell balloon (reference (b)) but slight differences indicate that it may have been made by another manufacturer. A close-up photograph of this assembly and its attachment to the envelope is shown in enclosure (B).

SHROUDS

6. The shroud lines are 1" circumference 3-strand manila ropes about 40 feet in length. They are identical in construction and attachment with those of the Kalispell balloon.

FUZE AND IGNITION CHARGE

7. The ignition charge is attached to the balloon between the equator and the skirt and consists of a charge of approximately 250 gm. of magnesium flash powder in a paper container 2" diameter by 5" long. A paper cord type fuze 36 feet in length leads to the ignition charge and shows no signs of having been lighted. However, since this section of fuze is considerably shorter than that found with the Kalispell paper balloon, it is probable that a portion of it is missing.

OTHER FUZES

8. Two burned fuzes, 32'8" and 31'8" in length were found with the balloon but were not attached to any part of the balloon assembly when received. The fuzes were impregnated with a tarry material and were wrapped with white cotton thread.

9. One end of each fuze leads into pieces of brass tubing 2" long by 5/16" O.D. (thickness about 1/64"). Around each of these tubes are grooved bakelite tubes 1-5/16" long by 1/16" thick, evidently for temperature insulation. The other ends of the fuzes lead to brass tips which are 1-21/32" long. A 9/16" portion of the tip is of 1/64" thickness by ¼" O.D. diameter brass tubing and is crimped to the fuze. The tip expands to 13/32" O.D. and then tapers uniformly to 11/32" O.D. at the end. This latter portion of the tip is about 1/32" in thickness. The thick middle portion of the tip is knurled.

RUBBER-ROPE SHOCK ABSORBER

10. The rubber shock absorber is the same as that found with the Kalispell balloon. The ropes from the lower end of the shock absorber lead to the remains of a metal framework.

11. The shock absorber assembly was stretched under measured loads and the results indicate that it would be ineffective for loads in excess of 125 pounds. This agrees roughly with the value found for the rubber shock-absorber from the Kalispell balloon.

C-EF37(455-LBL)
C 455-7/45

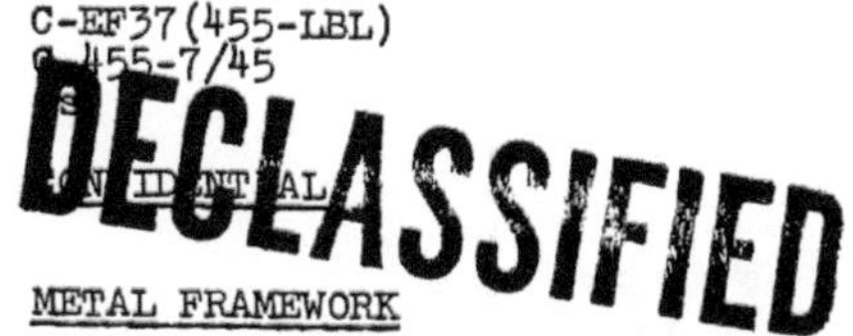

CONFIDENTIAL

METAL FRAMEWORK

12. The metal framework, as found, consists of three pieces of angle iron 7/8" x 12-7/8" x 1/32" connecting three iron posts - two 12" and one 6-3/4" long. A fourth 12" post, is tied to the rope assembly but its connection with the metal framework has been broken. The posts consist of two 5-½" sections of 12/32" diameter iron rod threaded on both ends and connected by means of a threaded hexagonal connector 1-3/8" long x 43/64" O.D. Cylindrical caps 1-1/2" long x 7/8" diameter are screwed onto the top of each post and are connected to the balloon by ropes passing through 3/8" holes drilled through the cap 7/16" from the top. The lower segments of three of the posts are broken off at the lower threads and the lower segment of the fourth is entirely missing. The posts pass through 25/64" holes in the pieces of angle iron 7/16" from the ends. Each post passes through two pieces of angle iron, one bent up and the other down, and the angle iron is held in position by means of hexagonal nuts which are screwed tightly against the cylindrical caps. The resulting framework is square in shape.

13. Pieces of bakelite 3/16" thick were found on two of the posts. The lower sections of the posts pass through holes in the bakelite and the pieces are held tightly against the hexagonal connectors by means of hexagonal nuts.

ELECTRICAL CONNECTIONS

14. Eleven rubber-covered wires, the longest piece 20" in length, are tied to one of the above posts in the metal framework by means of black friction tape. Two of these wires lead to a segment of a bakelite insulator 3/32" thick x 1-1/16" wide x 7-1/2" long which is evidently part of a bakelite circle about 1-1/16" wide x 24" diameter. The bakelite contains seven electrical contacts (small, female) spaced about 1" apart and connected in pairs. Another wire leads to a smaller segment of the same circle containing only three contacts, two of which are hooked together.

SOURCE AND PURPOSE.

15. The additional information secured through an examination of this balloon is insufficient to warrant changing any of the conclusions made in regard to the Kalispell balloon. The only evidence of any value is that the two balloons are identical in construction and this would indicate that they are not just experimental models.

NAVAL RESEARCH LABORATORY

S-EF37(455-HAT) Anacostia Station

S-455-8/45
Serial No. 4437
kos

Washington, D.C.

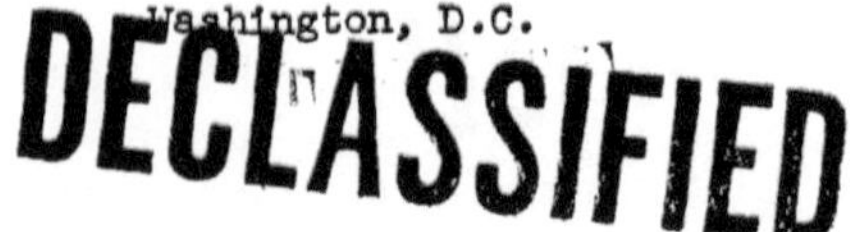

15 January 1945

To: Officer in Charge
Technical Air Intelligence Center
Naval Air Station
Anacostia, D. C.

Subj: Balloon and Appurtenances, Japanese, from Kailua, Hawaii.

Refs: (a) Conf. ltr CL-221320 of 22 December 1944 from Joint Intelligence Center, Pacific Ocean Areas to NRL.
(b) NRL ltr C-455-HAT of 8 January 1945 to TAIC, NAS, Anacostia on Kalispell Paper Balloon.
(c) NRL ltr C-EF37(455-HAT) of 9 January 1945 to TAIC, NAS, Anacostia on San Pedro Rubber Balloon.
(d) NRL ltr C-EF37(455-LBL) of 15 January 1945 to TAIC, NAS, Anacostia on Estacado Paper Balloon.

Encls: (HW)
(A) Photograph - Release Gear - Side View.
(B) " " " - Top View.
(C) " " " - Bottom View.
(D) " " " - Barometric Contactors.
(E) " " " - Trigger Switches.
(F) Sketch " " - Electrical and Fuze Connections.
(G) " - Balloon Assembly.

1. At the request of Ref:(a) the Laboratory has made a study of the subject balloon and appurtenances. It has been concluded that this balloon was a paper one virtually identical with those described in Refs:(b) and (d). This balloon, and probably the other two, carried an ingenious ballast release mechanism for maintaining an altitude in excess of 20,000 feet. This would permit a flight of considerable duration and thus increases the possibility that they were sent aloft in Japan rather than from a submarine. The ballast could be either inert material or incendiaries or the like. Apparently the balloon has carried little equipment other than the ballast release gear and ballast. The investigation is being continued and any further information of interest will be forwarded. A detailed analysis follows.

DISCOVERY.

2. At 1000 on 14 November 1944, the Coast Guard at Kailua, Hawaii, saw an airborne object descend into the sea 5 miles out. The object was reported to be a paper balloon 15 feet in diameter by a boat sent to retrieve it. A fragment of the envelope and some of the attached gear was recovered from 20 feet of water. After examination in Hawaii, the material was sent to NRL where it was received on 9 January 1944.

INVENTORY

3. The material received at NRL consisted of a fragment of a paper balloon, a fragment of shroud line, and an assembly of switches, fuzes, and barometric contactors apparently functioning as ballast release gear, and two 32.5 ft. long fuzes.

S-EF37(455-HAT)
S-455-8/45
Serial No. 4437
kos

ENVELOPE

4. The fragment of envelope received is from the skirt and matches in size, shape, material, and general appearance the corresponding sections of the Kalispell and Estacado balloons.

SHROUD LINE

5. The fragment of shroud line is identical with and carries a hook fastening identical with the corresponding parts of the Kalispell and Estacado balloons.

FUZES

6. The two 32-1/2 ft. fuzes were apparently identical with the short (22 inch) fuzes used in the ballast release gear. The burning rate of the latter is about 1 foot per minute. The long fuzes have at one end tapered plugs fitting the trigger switch mechanism of the release gear. At the other end they terminate in short brass tubes having plastic hand grips. The long fuzes were wrapped around the battery box when the gear was received at NRL.

BALLAST RELEASE GEAR

7. A side view of the ballast release gear is shown in Enclosure (A). Enclosure (B) shows a top view with the battery box cover removed and Enclosure (C) shows a bottom view. Enclosure (D) shows further details of the barometric contactors and Enclosure (E) is a close-up view of the trigger switch mechanism. The hook-up for the whole assembly is shown in Enclosure (F). The whole assembly as received weighed 15 pounds.

8. The release gear was supported by four pairs of ropes leading to the four pillars of the assembly. The balloon from Estacado (Ref:(d)) had attached to the shock absorber assembly four pairs of ropes leading to four similar pillars, three pieces of angle iron similar to those surrounding the battery box and several pieces of wire and two fragments of connector circles similar to the connector circles visible in Encl.(A). Apparently the Estacado balloon had a similar mechanism attached.

9. The battery assembly consisted of a small one-cell sulfuric acid type storage battery enclosed within three celluloid boxes and the whole enclosed in a wood box 11" by 11" by 6" deep. This rested on a bakelite disk and was held in place by strips of angle iron connecting the four pillars at the top.

10. The barometric contactors consisted of four barometric bellows arranged to form electrical contacts below a certain altitude and to break the contacts above that altitude. Each was covered by a pressed steel housing. Encl.(F) shows the hook-up. Three of the contactors were identical single cell bellows making direct contacts. The fourth differed in that it contained a two cell bellows and made contact through a friction clutch. As long as the balloon was ascending or stationary no contact was made. As soon as it dropped a predetermined amount from a maximum altitude, a contact would be made. Thus the number 4 element makes a contact when the balloon begins to descend regardless of altitude.

S-EF37(455-HAT)
S-455-8/45
Serial No. 4437
kos

11. The contactors were set for altitude as follows:

#1 - Not used - Adjustment screw adjusted so that no contact is made at any altitude.
#2 - Set to make a contact when the balloon descended below 3.9 miles and to break the contact when the altitude reached 4.1 miles.
#3 - Made contact below 3.6 miles and broke it above 4.0 miles.
#4 - Made a contact whenever the external pressure increased from any minimum by 40 mm. of mercury. This corresponds to a drop of 0.5 miles at 4.0 miles altitude or 0.8 miles at 6.0 miles.

12. The number 4 contactor would form a contact at any time the balloon descended and the number 2 and number 3 contactors would function if the balloon fell below 3.9 miles and 3.6 miles respectively. These three contactors are in parallel connection so that any one will close the circuit. Thus, there is a contact any time the balloon descends more than around 0.5 miles or any time it falls below 3.9 miles.

13. The contactors and the battery are connected with the remainder of the mechanism through a molded plastic connector. This is visible in Encls: (A) and (D) and the connections are shown in Encl:(F).

14. Immediately below the battery box is a plastic disk 19" in diameter having about its periphery 36 numbered pairs of electrical contacts. Immediately below this is a circular aluminum ring carrying 72 spring loaded plungers. Encl.(E) shows a close-up view of these "trigger switches". Each switch is restrained from closing by a tapered plug fitting into a hole in the aluminum ring and engaging a hook on the plunger. Each tapered plug contains an explosive charge and when the fuze on each plug ignites the charge, that plug is thrown out allowing the plunger to rise and close the circuit between the aluminum ring and that contact point on the plastic disk.

15. The base of the apparatus consists of an aluminum wheel 23-1/2" in diameter. The rim has 72 tapered holes to receive 72 tapered plugs. These plugs contain explosive charges to drive them out when they are electrically fired. Immediately above the rim of the wheel are three plastic rings holding in place 72 pairs of connectors for the plug leads. The fuze ends fit into the rim butting against the plugs so that the explosion of the plug also ignites the fuze. Encl.(C) shows this arrangement. At the center bottom of the wheel are two additional electrical fuze igniters. One has been used and the other has not. Apparently these fuzes would lead to the destructive ignition charge on the envelope.

16. The rim of the wheel contains a deep slot. It is presumed that wedge or "T"-shaped inserts fitted into this slot and rested on the plugs. Thus, whenever one or both of a pair of plugs blew out the object suspended on those plugs would be free to fall.

17. The cycle of operation would be as follows. On the ground the barometric contacts would be closed but no action would occur because all of the trigger switches are open. When the balloon is released the two long fuzes are lighted. They burn through in about 35 minutes and blow out their terminal plugs closing the first pair of switches. By this time the balloon is above 20,000 feet and rising so the barometric contacts are open and no further action occurs. When the balloon reaches a maximum altitude and then falls enough to close one of the barometric contacts, the first pair of plugs

S-EF37(455-HAT)
S-455-8/45
Serial No. 4437
kos

in the rim are fired allowing ballast to drop and lighting the fuzes leading to the number 2 pair of trigger switches. These fuzes require about 2 minutes to burn through and blow out their terminal plugs closing the second pair of trigger switches. If the balloon has in the meantime ascended enough to open the barometric contacts, no further action occurs. If the balloon has not risen enough the second pair of rim plugs blows out dropping a second portion of ballast and lighting the fuzes to the number 3 trigger switches. When the number 36 pair of trigger switches closes and one of the barometric contacts closes the fuze leading to the envelope is ignited to destroy the envelope. The unused number 1 barometric contactor and the unused fuze igniter connected to it could be used to destroy the envelope if the balloon fell below a set altitude at any time.

18. Tied to the bottom of the assembly are four pieces of twine, one of which has a 1-foot length of light steel wire attached. These pieces may have been used to fasten on additional gear or to hold arming wires. The weight of this additional gear could be as much as 50 pounds or more but in view of the fact that rope used elsewhere in the assembly is many times as strong as necessary, it is presumptive that any additional gear tied on did not exceed 10 pounds.

19. The objects released from the balloon could obviously be either inert ballast or some incendiary or similar device, or both. Release of the objects may be the primary purpose of the device. On the other hand it may have carried radiosonde equipment or some sort of plane detection or interference equipment, and the release of ballast is incidental to keeping the balloon aloft for a considerable period.

20. The presence of automatic ballast release equipment increases the possibility that the balloons are coming from a considerable distance, perhaps from Japan itself.

21. The purpose of the self destructive feature is apparently to avoid recovery of the equipment by the Allies or to avoid detection of the operation. This slightly favors the theory that radiosonde or plane detection equipment, rather than incendiaries, are involved. It is still in the realm of possibility that the ballast units might contain insect pests, disease germs, or the like.

22. The Laboratory has just received fragments of a fourth paper balloon from Sevastopol via Ft. Lewis, Washington. Preliminary examination indicates that this was identical in all respects, including the ballast release gear, to the other three paper balloons. With this gear were received the remains of three small incendiary charge containers.

23. The whole assembly of paper balloon, shrouds, shock absorber, and release gear are apparently a standard Japanese item. Encl.(G) shows a sketch of the whole assembly. This will be referred to in any further reports as the "standard Japanese paper balloon".

R. H. BULLARD
Comdr., USNR
By Direction of Director
Naval Research Laboratory

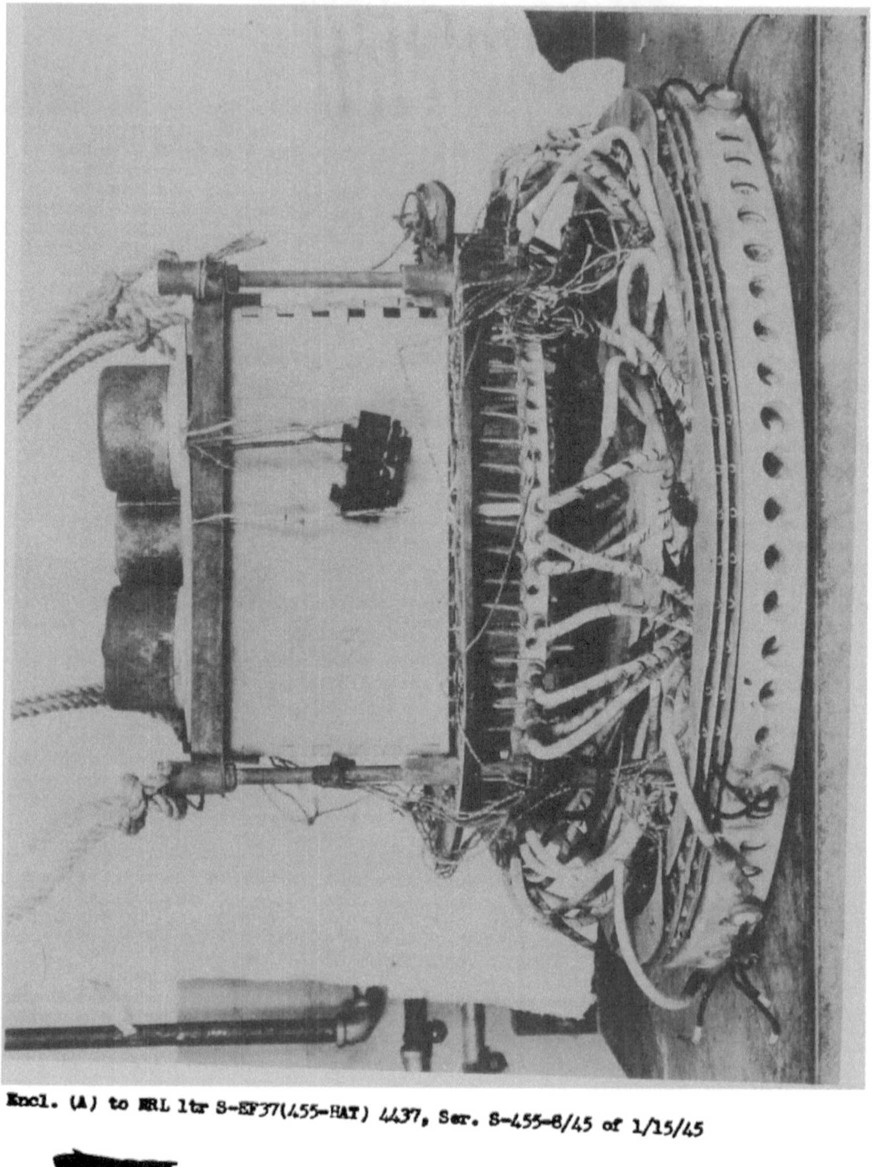

Encl. (A) to NRL ltr S-EF37(455-HAT) 4437, Ser. S-455-8/45 of 1/15/45

DECLASSIFIED

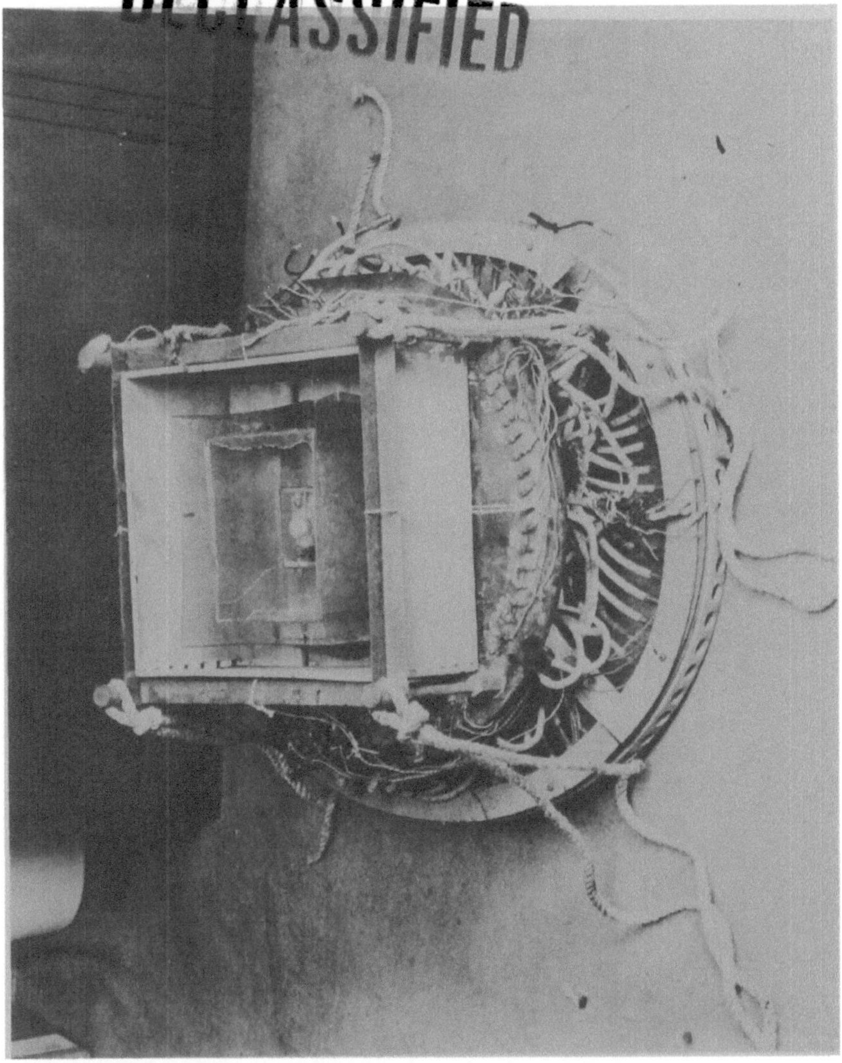

Encl. (B) to NRL ltr S-NP37(455-HAT) 4437, Ser. #B-455-8/45 of 1/15/45

25

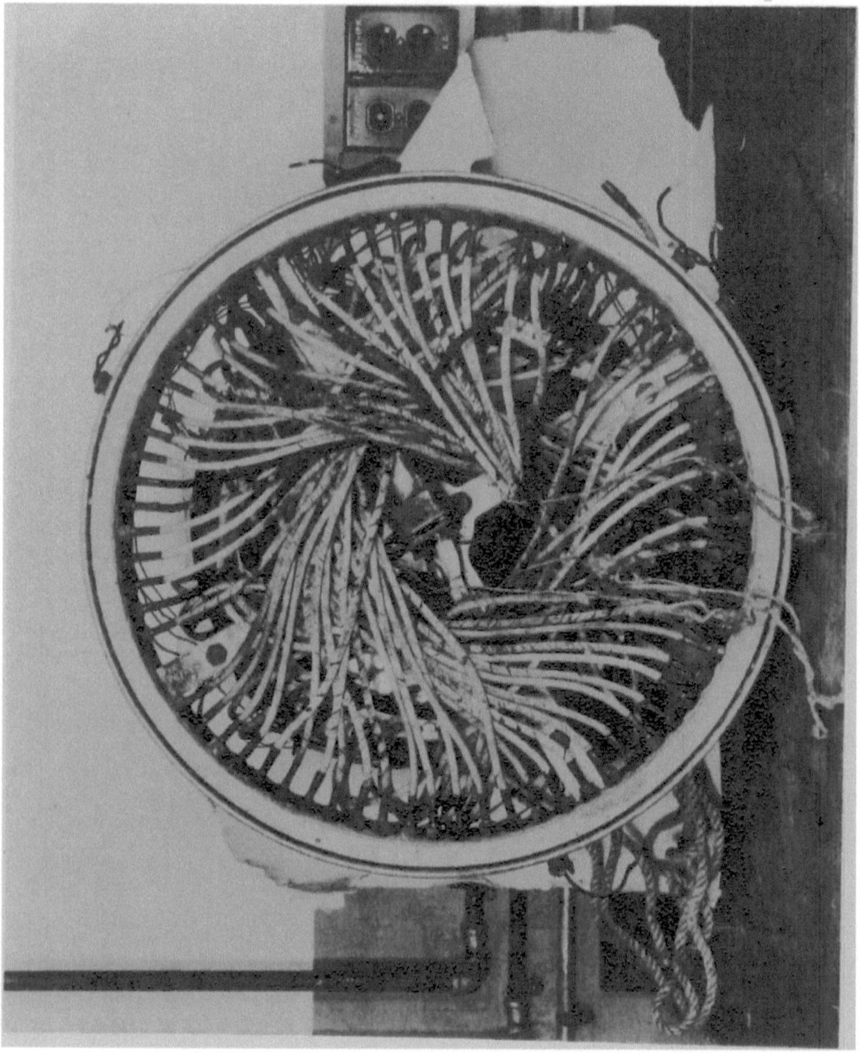

Encl. (C) to NRL ltr S-EF37(455-HAT) 4437, Ser. S-455-8/45 of 1/15/45

DECLASSIFIED

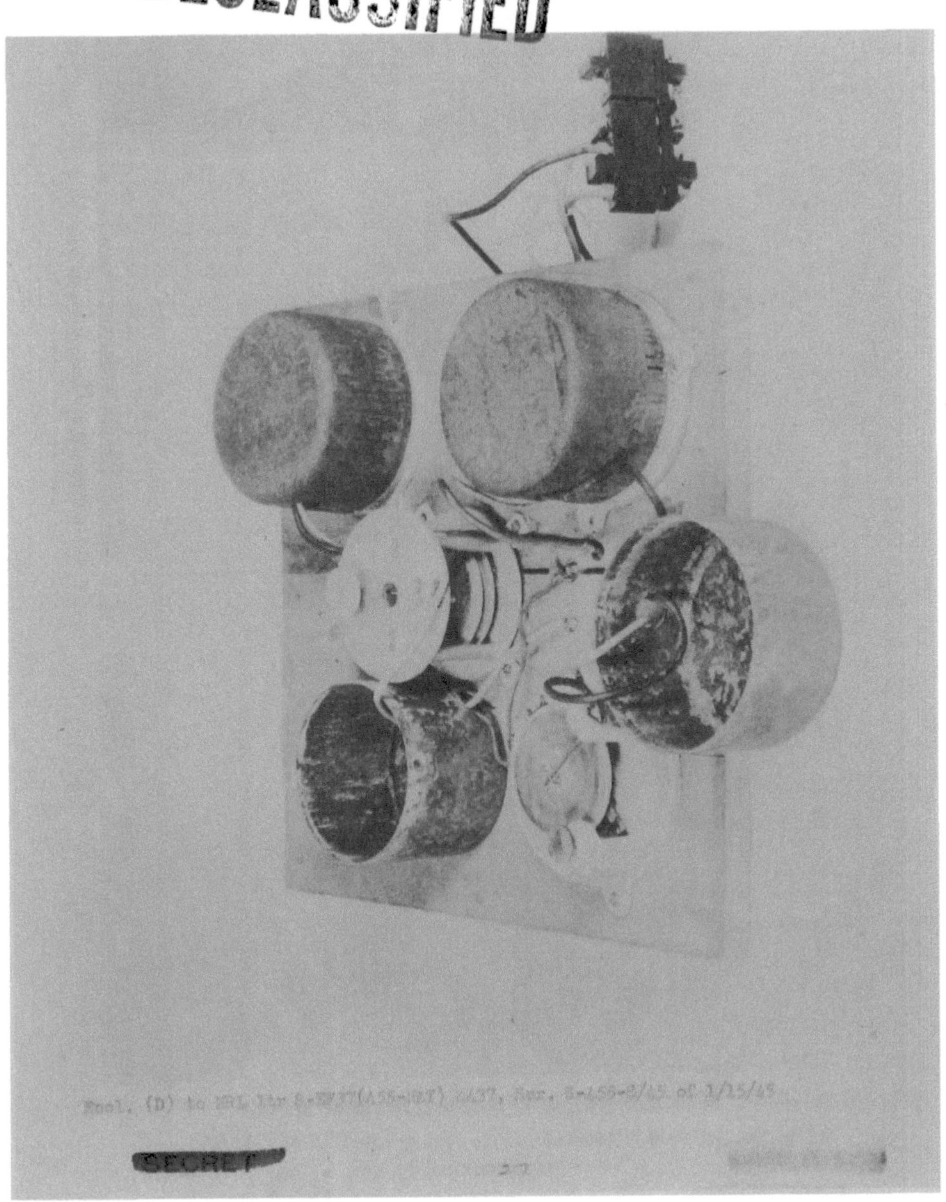

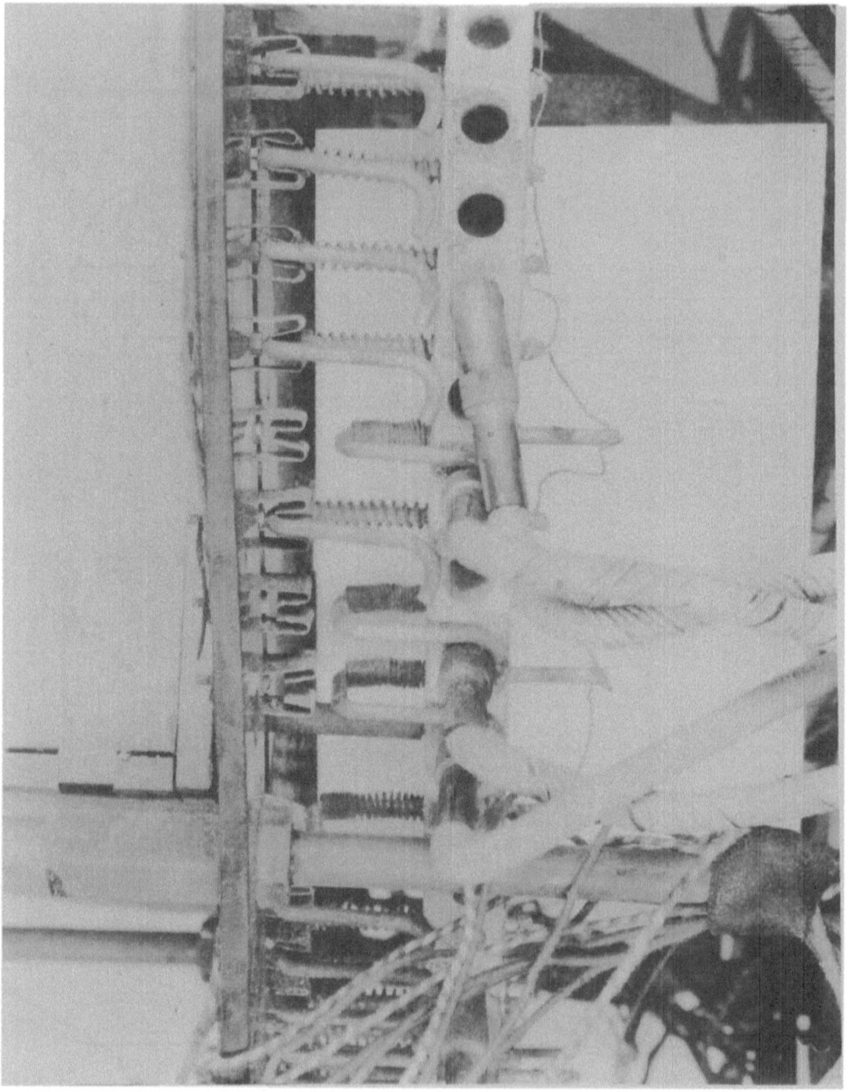

Encl. (E) to NRL ltr S-EF37(455-HAT) 4437, Ser. S-455-8/45 of 1/15/45

28

#1 (not used)

#2

#3

#4

↑ Barometric Kontactors

− Bat. +

←Plug Connector

↓Trigger Switches

#1 #2 #3 #36

(not used)

Fuze to Envelope

#1 #2 #3 #36

↑ Blow-out Plugs and interval fuzes.

32.5 Ft. Fuzes

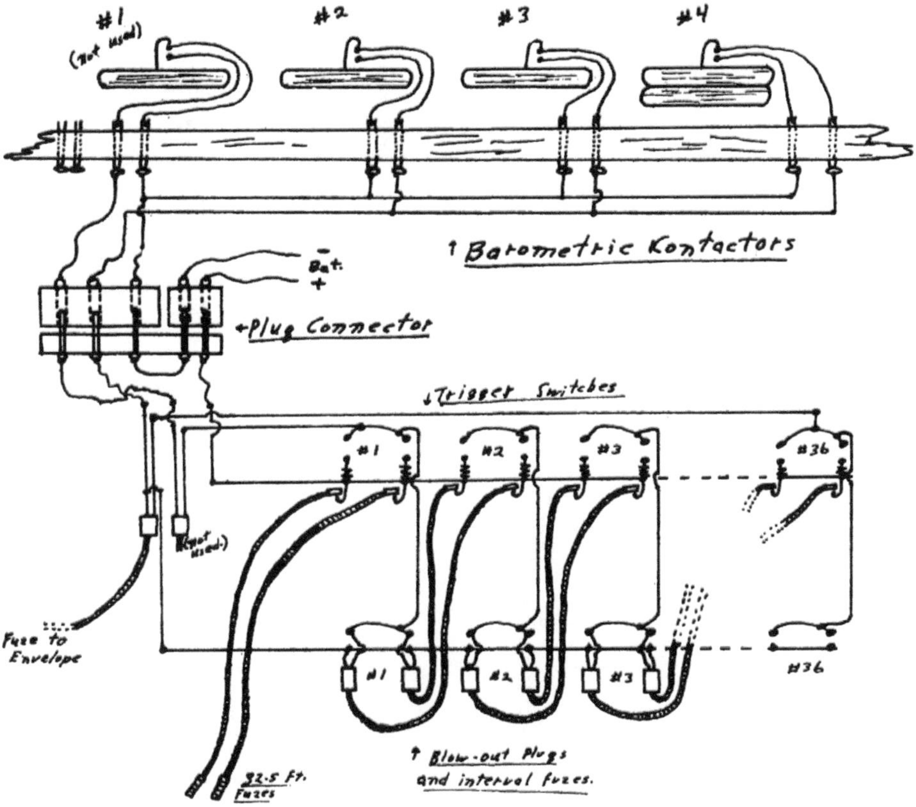

Electrical and Fuze Connections in Release Gear

Enclosure F.

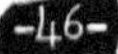

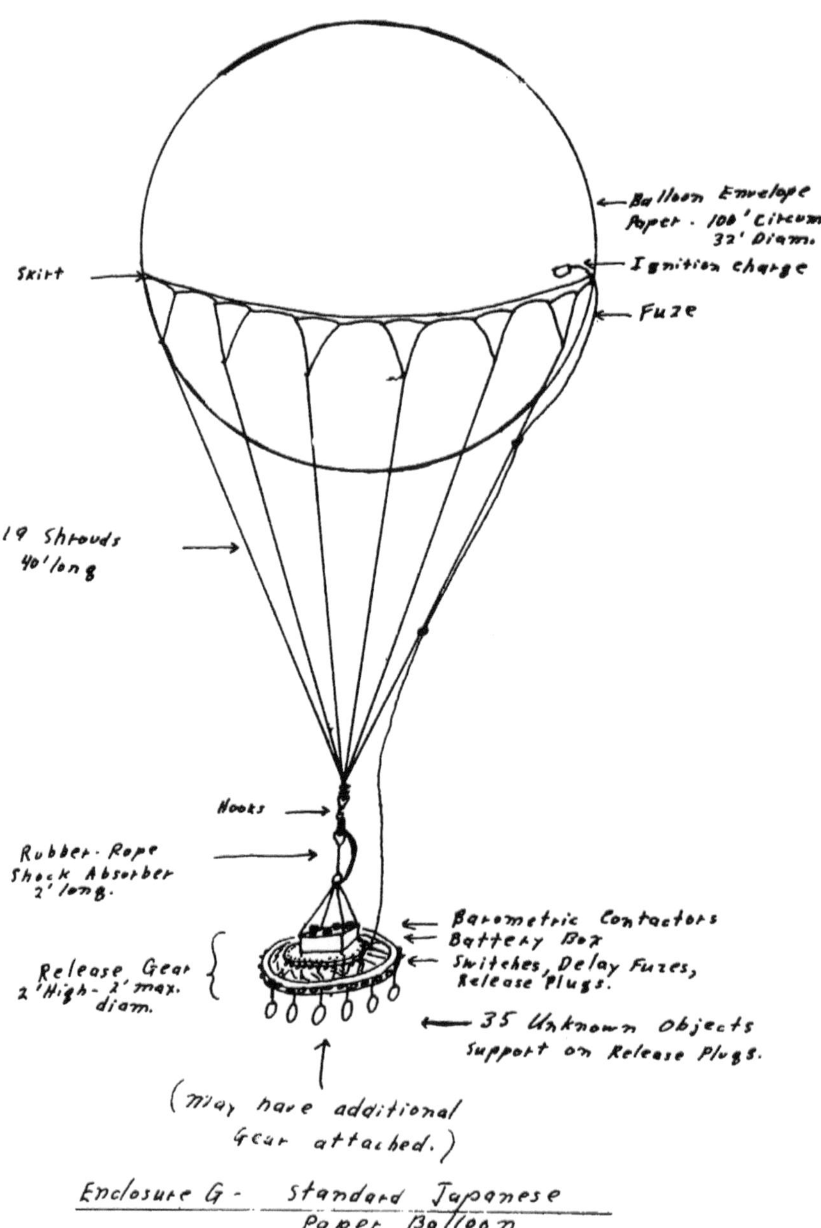

Enclosure G - Standard Japanese Paper Balloon

NAVAL RESEARCH LABORATORY

S-EF37(455-HAT)

Serial No. 4447
S-455-9/45
as

Anacostia Station
Washington 20, D. C.

DECLASSIFIED

18 January 1945

To: Officer in Charge of Technical Air Intelligence
Room 1W32
Navy Department
Washington 25, D. C.

Subj: Balloon remnants, Japanese, from Sevastopol via Ft. Lewis, Washington, CEE Nos. 22166, 22167, 22168.

Refs: (a) Visit of Lt.(jg) C. L. Miller of TAIC, NAS, Anacostia to NRL 12 January 1945.
(b) NRL ltr S-EF37(455-HAT) S-455-8/45 of 15 January to TAIC, NAS, Anacostia.
(c) NRL ltr C-455-HAT, C-455-5/45 of 8 January to TAIC, NAS, Anacostia.

1. At the request of the Technical Air Intelligence Center (reference (a)) the Laboratory has examined the subject balloon remnants. It has been determined that they are from a balloon identical with the "standard Japanese paper balloon" described in reference (b). The subject material also contained the remains of four incendiary bombs. It is now presumable that the Japanese have succeeded in designing a balloon which can be produced in large numbers at low cost and which is capable of reaching the United States and Canada from the western Pacific carrying incendiaries or other devices. The balloon envelope, made of paper, supports a ballast release mechanism which maintains the altitude in excess of 20,000 feet by releasing ballast when necessary. The ballast can be inert material for the earlier part of the trip and incendiaries or other devices during the final part of the trip. The latter will be scattered along over a distance of many miles. The balloon envelope is destroyed by an ignition charge which is ignited when the final portion of ballast is released. A detailed analysis of the material from Sevastopol follows.

DISCOVERY

2. No information has been received at NRL regarding the discovery of this material. It was sent from Sevastopol via Ft. Lewis, Washington to the Technical Air Intelligence Center, NAS, Anacostia and brought to NRL on 12 January 1945 for examination.

INVENTORY

3. The items received at NRL included the skirt from the balloon envleope, the shroud lines, the remains of the envelope ignition charge, 60 feet of unfired fuze, two 32-ft. lengths of fired fuze, supporting ropes for the ballast release gear, the ballast rèlease gear (badly damaged), the remains of four incendiary charges, and about 200 cc of snow packed in dry ice.

SKIRT

4. The skirt consisted of the rope loops and fragments of paper and was identical with the corresponding parts of the other paper balloons, (reference (b)).

DECLASSIFIED

S-EF37(455-HAT)
Serial No. 4447
S-455-9/45
as

SHROUDS

5. The shrouds were identical with those from the other paper balloons (reference (b)). They were in a newer condition than any previously received.

IGNITION CHARGE

6. The ignition charge consisted of magnesium flash powder in a cylindrical paper container with a fuze leading to it. It was identical with those previously examined.

SIXTY-FOOT FUZE

7. This fuze leads from the ballast release gear to the ignition charge on the envelope (reference (b)). It was received as a separate length of fuze and was unfired.

THIRTY-TWO FOOT FUZES

8. Two fired fuzes 32 feet in length with tapered plugs at one end and hand grips at the other end were received. These are used to initiate the action of the ballast release gear (reference (b)).

BALLAST RELEASE GEAR

9. The ballast release gear was badly damaged but apparently identical with that described in reference (b). The altitude settings of the four barometric contactors were as follows:

- #1. Contact made at 3.8 miles descending and broken at 5.3 miles ascending. (Slightly damaged).
- #2. Contact made at 4.6 miles descending and broken at 4.65 miles ascending.
- #3. Contact made at 4.3 miles descending and broken at 5.3 miles ascending.
- #4. Contact made when balloon descends 0.5 miles at 4 miles or when it descends 0.8 miles at 6 miles.

10. In this instance the #1 bellows and both fuze igniters for the envelope fuze had been used. The #1 bellows and one igniter were unused on the Kailua balloon (see paragraph 16 of reference (b)). One of the fuze igniters had attached to it a 5-foot length of fuze identical with the envelope ignition charge fuze. This was burned half way through starting at the igniter end. It is not yet certain that the fuze ignited by the #1 bellows is connected with the envelope ignition charge. It may lead to some independent self-destructive device.

11. At the bottom of the ballast release gear was attached a 1-foot length of twine and on this was a 15-inch length of light steel wire resembling an arming wire. The Kailua release gear carried four pieces of twine, one of which held an arming wire.

S-EF37(455-HAT)
Serial No. 4447
S-455-9/45
as

INCENDIARY CHARGES

12. No information was received on the relationship of these charges to the other items. One consisted of a heavy gauge (1/8 inch) pressed steel container 3-3/4 inches in diameter and 7 inches deep. It contained a fused metallic mass inside and was burned through around the top. The container had been subjected to a high temperature. At the top center was the remains of what had probably been an impact fuze. Around the top was a metal strap extended to form a lug. Linked to the lug was a steel hook identical with the peculiarly shaped hooks used to connect the shroud lines to the skirt. This suggests that the incendiary may have been attached to the release gear using a short piece of rope and a suitable fitting to engage in the release gear. The weight of this item as received was 4 Kgs.

13. A second incendiary was of much lighter steel (.018-inch wall thickness) and 3-3/4 inches in diameter and 9 inches deep. It contained charred wood and fused metallic material and was burned through at some points. The weight as received was 1-1/4 Kgs.

14. The pulverized remains of two other incendiary charges were received. In a separate envelope was received a cylindrical solid metal plunger (1/2-inch diameter by 1 inch long) having a pointed coaxial projection at one end. It is highly probable that this is the plunger from an impact fuze.

SNOW

15. Examination of the snow indicates that it contains material from the storage battery cell. The latter was badly damaged when received.

SOURCE AND PURPOSE

16. In prior reports on the Japanese paper balloons, and particularly in reference (c), certain deductions have been made as to source and purpose. In view of the larger amount of information now available it is advisable to reexamine this phase of the problem. The NRL has now received parts of four paper balloons. A fifth has been reported enroute from Alaska. Since the balloons have a self-destructive device probably only a small percentage land intact and of these only a small percentage would be discovered. It must therefore be assumed that a considerable number are coming over. This argues against their being launched from submarines. The use of an automatic ballast release makes possible a sustained flight and the ballast release devices have been exhausted on the balloons recovered indicating that they have come a considerable distance. It seems fairly certain that the balloons are coming from Japan. In reference (a) an air current moving from Japan via Hawaii to Montana at 25,000 feet was described. Reports from other sources including the B-29 planes operating over Japan have verified the existence of strong westerly winds at that altitude.

17. The presence of automatic ballast release equipment rules out the theory that personnel are being carried.

18. The great number which are apparently being sent up indicates that radiosonde is not the prime purpose.

19. The use of an automatic ballast release to obtain a sustained flight indicates that air raid detection or prevention is not the objective since the balloons would very quickly be carried away from the theatre of operations by air currents.

20. Many of the components have definitely been made by mass production methods. Minor differences between the various balloons show that some production short-cuts and simplifications have been introduced indicating that manufacturing experience has developed. There is no apparent reason why these balloons could not be produced in very large quantities.

21. The use of a self-destructive feature in conjunction with the ballast release mechanism must have been intended to prevent the recovery of any balloons in this country.

22. From the above considerations, it is evident that the Japanese have purposefully designed a balloon which can be produced in large quantities and which is capable of being carried across the Pacific to release incendiaries or other devices in this country. They are probably well along in their production plans and are sending over a considerable number already. It is to be expected that the number will increase and that when the dry season arrives considerable damage will result unless effective countermeasures are developed.

R. H. BULLARD
Comdr., USNR
By Direction of Director
Naval Research Laboratory

NAVAL RESEARCH LABORATORY

S-EF37(455-HAT)

Anacostia Station

S-455-12/45
Serial No. 4475

Washi[illegible] D.C.

[redacted]

1 February 1945

To: Officer in Charge
Technical Air Intelligence Center
Naval Air Station
Anacostia, D.C.

Subj: Balloon, Japanese Paper, from Marshall, Alaska, CEE 22179.

Refs:
(a) Visit of Lt.(jg) C. L. Miller of TAIC, NAS, Anacostia to NRL on 18 Jan. 1945.
(b) NRL ltr S-EF37(455-HAT), S-455-8/45 of 15 Jan. 1945 to TAIC, NAS, Anacostia.
(c) NRL ltr C-EF37(455-LBL), C-455-7/45 of 15 Jan. 1945 to TAIC, NAS, Anacostia.
(d) NRL ltr S-EF37(455-HAT), S-455-9/45 of 20 Jan. 1945 to TAI, Navy Dept., Wash., D.C.
(e) NRL ltr C-455-HAT, C-455-5/45 of 8 Jan. 1945 to TAIC, NAS, Anacostia.

1. At the request of the Technical Air Intelligence Center, NAS, Anacostia, (Ref.(a)), the Laboratory has examined the subject balloon remnants. They have been identified as parts of the standard Japanese paper balloon described in Ref.(b). Apparently the use of a long fuze and an ignition charge on the envelope to accomplish self-destruction has been replaced by the use of a short length of fuze leading to an explosive charge on the ballast release gear. Remains of three sand bag ballast units were identified. Two arming wires were found on the release gear and a length of twine, which may have carried a third. The most probable altitude for such a balloon reaching the west coast has been calculated from the ballast weight to be 35,000 to 45,000 feet.

DISCOVERY

2. The subject material was recovered 15 miles south of Marshall, Alaska on 10 January 1945. It was believed to have landed on 23 December 1944.

INVENTORY

3. The material received at NRL included three large sections of the balloon envelope, the relief valve, remains of the ballast release gear and its supporting ropes, two 32-foot lengths of fired fuze, the remains of the storage battery and battery boxes, the remains of the barometric contactor assembly and two sand filled ballast bags.

ENVELOPE

4. The envelope apparently was the usual paper sphere as described in Ref.(b) and earlier reports. There was no evidence of the use of an ignition charge on the envelope.

RELIEF VALVE

5. The relief valve was identical with that on the Estacado balloon (Ref.(c)). The number "93" was painted on in two places. A large number "26" had been written on in chalk. Stamped on the valve spring support was the number "2569". The Estacado valve was re-examined and found to have the number

"2647", in the same position. The Kalispell valve, which is slightly different, had no number stamped on it, but the number "1241" was painted on. This was inadvertently omitted from the report on the Kalispell balloon. It is possible that the four digit numbers are serial numbers while the others are to identify workmen, or for production records or some similar use. There were no rope loops on this valve.

BAROMETRIC CONTACTORS

6. The barometric contactors were set as follows:

#1 made contact at 2.28 miles descending and broke contact at 2.30 miles ascending.
#2 made contact at 2.9 miles descending and broke contact at 3.7 miles ascending.
#3 made contact at 1.7 miles descending and broke contact at 2.5 miles ascending.
#4 not in operating condition.

These are lower values than obtained with the Kailua and Sevastopol balloons (Ref.(b) and (d)). The number 4 contactor either was damaged in landing or was improperly assembled. The friction clutch between the expansion element and the contact arm is disengaged in such a fashion as to indicate improper assembly rather than subsequent damage. All of the contactors were badly corroded. They carried the following markings:

#1 - "4000" in pencil
#2 - "7800" in pencil, "8" in chalk
#3 - "8" in chalk
#4 - "700" in pencil

BATTERY ASSEMBLY

7. The battery was the usual one cell storage battery housed inside three plastic boxes and a wood box. Ref.(b) shows a photograph of the battery and boxes. The battery is enclosed in a tight fitting plastic case and the space between this and the next larger box is filled with a 10% solution of calcium chloride. Apparently the calcium chloride solution is intended to act as a heat reservoir to keep the battery from getting too cold. The solution would tend to hold the battery at around 0°C to -20°C until the solution had completely frozen. The battery and the surrounding solution are insulated from the outside air by a double air space on the sides and top. On the bottom there are no air spaces since each box rests on the bottom of the next larger box. The leat insulation on the bottom is therefore nil. This is of interest because the ballast release gear apparently failed to function due to a failure in the current supply. One of the two #21 trigger switches had closed and the lead from these switches to the #21 plugs was intact but neither plug had fired. Both center plugs were unfired and one should have fired during the descent when the number 1 barometric contactor closed.

8. A test of the battery, as received, showed it to have an e.m.f. of about 1.4 volts. A current of 0.53 amperes at 0.52 volts was found to be sufficient to fire one of the blow-out plugs (aluminum) and 0.36 amperes at 0.45 volts was sufficient to fire another (steel). The filaments in the blow-out plugs have resistances of 0.80-0.81 ohms when cold and 1.0-1.25 ohms when heated to the firing temperature. The failure of the plugs to detonate even though the electrical circuit was closed may be due to either of two possibilities (1) mechanical failure of some other part of the electrical system, or (2) freezing of the solution in the battery whereby its capacity becomes too low to heat the filaments. This second possibility also requires that the

electrical contacts be permanently broken before the battery has a chance to thaw, otherwise the release mechanism would start working again. Presumably the balloon could crash before the battery warmed up. The batteries received to date have had the acid spilled out. The usual battery acid however freezes at around -30°F.

RELEASE GEAR

9. The release gear was identical in construction with that described in Ref.(b). The pairs of blow-out plugs from number 21 to number 35 inclusive had not fired. Each of the unfired pairs supported a "T" shaped flat iron bracket. A hook attached to each of the brackets and the sand bags were attached to the hooks. This is the arrangement deduced in Ref.(b). The hooks are the same peculiar shaped hooks used to attach the shrouds to the envelope. Apparently all 35 pairs were laden with sand bags only. The two blow-out plugs at the center bottom of the release mechanism also supported a "T" shaped bracket somewhat heavier than the others. No attachment remained on this bracket but it is obviously intended for the cargo, perhaps an incendiary such as those from Sevastopol (Ref.(d)). Attached to the bottom of the release gear were three 1-foot lengths of twine, two of which had attached steel arming wires about 15 inches long.

10. The bottom center blow-out plugs, which were unfired, ignite two fuzes which in the previous balloons lead to the ignition charge on the envelope. In this instance one of these fuzes is 24 inches long and terminates in a cylindrical brass detonator 2-1/2 inches long and 5/16 inch in diameter. The other fuze was missing and apparently had been pulled out, perhaps when the balloon dragged across the earth in landing. The detonator was shiny uncorroded brass, suggesting that it had been encased in some material or device up to the time of landing. It is possible that the Japanese, having learned that the long fuze leading to an igniter on the envelope fails, have replaced it with a short fuze and a demolition charge.

11. The ballast release gear was supported by four doubled lengths of rope leading to the four pillars of the assembly. There was no indication that a rubber shock absorber had been used.

WIRING DIAGRAM OF BALLAST RELEASE GEAR

12. The wiring diagram of the ballast release mechanism is the same as that of Encl.(F), Ref.(b), with one exception. This diagram shows a wire leading from one of the central blow-out plugs to the first pair of trigger switches. This should be corrected to show this as a connection between the blow-out plug and the ninth pair of trigger switches. Thus, if the fuze trains fail anytime after the ninth pair of switches is activated, a decrease in altitude by the balloon will activate the detonator in one of the central blow-out plugs resulting in the dropping of the load attached there and (probably) demolition of the balloon.

BALLAST

13. The ballast consists of sand-filled paper bags about 10" x 3-1/2" x 3-1/2". When received the sand was wet and the pieces of ballast weighted 6-1/2 pounds each. The dry weight is 5-1/2 pounds each. The bag is made of the same kind of paper as the envelope of the balloon. The sand consists of a mixture of coarse, irregular shaped black and white particles and is a type that might be expected from volcanic rock of intermediate composition. The absence of shell material and the large proportion of sharp angular pieces indicate that it probably is not beach material. The dominant

portion of the sand is composed of quartz but there are also present considerable amounts of pyroxenes, potassium and lime soda feldspars and small amounts of tourmaline and garnet.

14. The bag is supported by two loops of two ply 3/8" circumference manila rope which cross beneath the bag and are tied together at the top of the bag. The ropes are fastened to the sides of the bag by paper patches. From the top of the bags, the ropes lead to hooks by which the ballast is attached to the ballast release gear.

FUZES

15. The two 32' burned fuzes are the same as those found with several of the other balloons and described in Ref.(b). They are evidently ignited on the ground but do not arm the ballast release mechanism until sufficient time has passed for the balloon to have reached a high altitude.

FLIGHT CHARACTERISTICS

16. It is now possible to make a better estimate of the flight characteristics of these balloons. Assuming that the original ballast load consisted of 35 bags identical with those recovered, the starting weight tally is as follows:

Weight of envelope	-	152 pounds
Weight of valve	-	10 pounds
Weight of shrouds	-	20 pounds
Weight of release gear	-	15 pounds
Weight of ballast	-	192 pounds
Total	-	389 pounds

17. This would not include the weight of the bomb, incendiary, or other item suspended from the bottom center plugs in the released gear. Assuming 20 pounds as a reasonable value based on the size of the center plugs and "T" brackets compared to those supporting the ballast the total weight becomes 409 pounds. This makes the initial ceiling 33,000 feet (Ref. (e)). The minimum altitude setting or altitude at which ballast is released has varied on the three sets of release gear examined to date. The highest minimum altitude setting on any of the three was 25,000 feet (Ref.(d)). If we assume that the balloon is intended to operate at 30,000 feet ceiling and 25,000 feet floor, when released the weight of the bomb or other attachment would have to be about 55 pounds. It is not likely that the altitude ceiling and "floor" would be closer together than 5,000 feet. If this difference were reduced to 2,000 feet the weight of the attachment could be as much as 90 pounds. The balloons as released would therefore operate under a ceiling of 27,000 to 33,000 feet and above a "floor" depending on the adjustment of the barometric contactors. The "floor" settings on the three sets of contactors so far recovered are as follows:

Sevastopol Balloon	- 25,000 feet	(Ref.(d))
Kailua Balloon	- 20,000 feet	(Ref.(b))
Marshall Balloon	- 15,000 feet	(Paragraph 6 above)

18. The balloon in flight will be at its ceiling altitude most of the time. It will cruise at the ceiling altitude until forced 300 feet below the ceiling through temperature effects or vertical air current components. It will then descend, release ballast, and reascend. The ceiling will become higher each time ballast is released. Assuming a 20 pound attachment the balloon will reach an ultimate ceiling of 46,000 feet. If the attachment weighs

S-EF37(455-HAT)
S-455-12/45
Serial No. 4475

90 pounds the ultimate ceiling will be 40,000 feet. The most probable altitude for a balloon reaching the west coast would be at 35,000 to 45,000 feet. Below this altitude the balloon will be ascending or descending or it will have crossed under such undisturbed atmospheric conditions that only a small amount of ballast has been released.

R. H. BULLARD
Comdr., USNR
By Direction of Director
Naval Research Laboratory

NAVAL RESEARCH LABORATORY
Anacostia Station
Washington 20, D.C.

S-EF37(455-HAT)

S-455-28/45
Secret Ser. 4587

2 March 1945

To: Officer in Charge,
Technical Air Intelligence Center,
U. S. Naval Air Station
Anacostia, D.C.

Subj: Balloon, Japanese Paper, from Holy Cross, Alaska.
CEE No. 22196.

Refs:
(a) Visit of Lt.(jg) C.L. Miller, TAIC, NAS, Anacostia to NRL on 8 Feb. 1945.
(b) NRL ltr. S-EF37(455-HAT), S-455-8/45 of 15 Jan. 1945 to TAIC, NAS, Anacostia.
(c) NRL ltr S-EF37(455-HAT), S-455-12/45 of 1 Feb. 1945 to TAIC, NAS, Anacostia.
(d) Western Defense Command CG, G-2 Conf. ltr. No. B-0211 to War Dept., G-2, dated 6 Feb. 1945 Forwarded by OPNAV to NRL on 9 Feb. 1945. Ser. 026383.

1. At the request of the Technical Air Intelligence Center, NAS, Anacostia (Ref.(a)), the Laboratory has examined the subject balloon material. The material has been identified as parts of the envelope, valve, shrouds, and ballast release mechanism from a Japanese paper balloon of the type described in Ref.(b). The principle difference found between this and previous balloons was that the ballast units recovered were lighter in weight and filled with a different kind of sand. The only previous ballast bags examined at this laboratory were from the Marshall, Alaska, balloon (Ref.(c)), and weighed 5.5 pounds each. The ballast bag with the present balloon was smaller in size and weighed 1.5 pounds.

DISCOVERY

2. The subject material was found at Holy Cross, Alaska. It was received at NRL on 8 February 1945.

INVENTORY

3. The material received at NRL consisted of several large sections of the envelope, the relief valve, the shrouds, a 60 ft. length of fuze, part of the ballast release mechanism, a bottle of liquid, and one unit of ballast. A rubber shock absorber was attached to the ballast release mechanism.

ENVELOPE

4. The envelope was apparently of the same size and construction as in the other balloons of this type. The material also appears to be the same. Some of the tape used on the seams was a light blue-green color. Because of the fragmentary conditon it was not possible to determine whether an envelope ignition charge was used. Since a long fuze was received with the balloon it is presumable that such an ignition charge was used.

VALVE

5. The valve was of the type found on the Kalispell and Alturas balloons. Painted on it was the number 1266.

S-EF37(455-HAT)
S-455-28/45
Secret Ser. 4587

SHROUDS

6. The shrouds were in a very weathered condition but otherwise no different from those on previous balloons.

LONG FUZE

7. The long fuze consisted of roughly 60 feet of cord type fuze identical with that used on previous balloons to set off the envelope ignition charge. It had burned about half way through and stopped at a point where the fuze was broken and held together only by some of the outer wrappings.

BALLAST RELEASE MECHANISM

8. This mechanism closely resembled that described in Ref.(b). It was supported on a rubber and rope shock absorber assembly similar to those found with the Kalispell and Estacado balloons. The barometric contactors and the battery were not received. Two pairs of ballast release plugs, #25 and #26, were unfired. One pair carried the usual "T" bracket for attaching ballast. The ballast bag received had a "T" attached and it is presumed that this was removed from the other pair of plugs after discovery. The failure of these two pairs to function was caused by a mistake in fuze arrangement. One fuze from the #24 plugs lead to a #27 switch instead of a #25 switch. The fuze which should have led from the #26 plugs to the #27 switch lead instead to a #25 switch. The second fuze leading from the #24 plugs to the #25 switches failed to light when the plug blew out. In addition to the failure of one #24 fuze to light similar failures occured on one #12 fuze, one #20 fuze, and one #27 fuze. One of the #30 fuzes ignited but went out. Both center plugs apparently had fired and blown out. The fuze leading from one was about a foot long and burned. The fuze from the other center plug was about two feet long, unburned, and had a cut end. Possibly the burned fuze had led to the envelope ignition charge and the unburned fuze had led to a demolition charge. Wrapped about the battery box were the two usual 16 foot starting fuzes. There were no arming wires nor was there any evidence that any had been attached.

BALLAST BAG

9. A single bag of sand ballast was received. This was smaller than those from the previous Alaska balloon and the weight, allowing for spillage, was about 1.5 pounds. The sand was quite different from that previously found (Ref.(c)) in that it consisted principally of orange-yellow particles with a few black and transparent particles whereas the Marshall, Alaska sand was a mixture of black and transparent particles resembling a mixture of salt and pepper.

10. The flight characteristics of these balloons and the maximum pay load were calculated in Ref.(c) assuming that all ballast units weighed 5-1/2 pounds each. If the ballast units are lighter the initial operating ceiling or the maximum pay load will be increased. Ref.(d) discloses that a ballast release mechanism from Hayfork, California, carried four bombs weighing respectively 10.5; 10.75; 10.5; and 11.1 pounds and seven sand bags weighing respectively 4.75; 4.375; 2.5; 2.25; 2.375; 2.5; and 6.75 pounds. Possibly undersized ballast bags are used in combination with the incendiary bombs in order to obtain a constant total load. The four bombs found are over a 5.5 pound average by a total of 20.8 pounds and the sand bags recovered are under a 5.5 pound average by 17.2 pounds disregarding the last bag which weighed 6.75 pounds. Based on a 6.75 average the four bombs are over by 15.9 pounds and the sand bags are under by 21.4 pounds. Ref. (c) reports one barometric contactor (aneroid) set at 35,000 feet. This would indicate that a higher initial ceiling was intended and that the average weight of the ballast bags.

S-EF37(455-HAT)
S-455-28/45
Secret Ser. 4587

or the weight of the pay load, was decreased. It is unfortunate that the barometric contactors on the Holy Cross balloon were not recovered as this would have provided a further clew as to whether the lighter ballast bags were to obtain a higher ceiling or to compensate for an increased pay load or the use of incendiaries as part of the ballast.

LIQUID

11. The liquid was water containing some calcium chloride and was probably from the battery box. The plastic box enclosing the battery which is the container for the calcium chloride solution was not received.

R. H. BULLARD
Comdr., USNR
By Direction of Director
Naval Research Laboratory

NAVAL RESEARCH LABORATORY

S-EF37(455-HAT)

Anacostia Station

S-455-29/45
Secret Ser. 4629

Washington 20, D. C.

2 March 1945

To: Officer in Charge,
Technical Air Intelligence Center,
Naval Air Station
Anacostia, D.C.

Subj: Balloon, Japanese Paper, from Alturas, California; CEE No. 22206.

Refs: (a) Visit of Lt(jg) C.L. Miller of TAIC, NAS, Anacostia to NRL on 6 Feb. 1945.
(b) NRL ltr. S-EF37(455-HAT), S-455-8/45 of 15 Jan. 1945 to TAIC.
(c) NRL ltr. S-EF37(455-HAT), S-455-30/45 of 16 Feb. 1945 to TAIC.

1. At the request of the Technical Air Intelligence Center, NAS, Anacostia (Ref.(a)) the Laboratory has examined the subject balloon material. It was found to consist of the envelope, valve, and shrouds from a Japanese Paper Balloon similar to the one described in Ref. (b).

DISCOVERY

2. This balloon was discovered at Alturas, California. It was received at NRL on 6 February 1945.

INVENTORY

3. The material received at NRL consisted of the balloon envelope, the relief valve, and part of the shrouds.

ENVELOPE

4. The envelope was a paper sphere similar in size and construction to those previously examined (Ref.(b)). Some of the tape used on the seams has a faint blue-green color. The paper is apparently the same as in the other balloons. There was no evidence of the use of an envelope incendiary however certain parts of the envelope had been removed.

VALVE

5. The valve was similar to those on the Kalispell and Holy Cross, Alaska balloons. A photograph of this valve and a discussion of the two kinds of valves will be found in Ref.(c). The valve had a painted 3060 and 42 in chalk written on it. There were rope loops on this valve. These loops were not present on the Marshall, Alaska balloon valve but have been found on all the other valves. They were not used on this balloon. The purpose is to help support the weight of the valve by means of light lines running to rope loops around the base of the envelope.

SHROUDS

6. The shrouds were badly frayed and tangled but apparently the same in arrangement as in previous balloons. With the shrouds was the rope assembly used to hook the ballast release mechanism to the shrouds, consisting of 8

S-EF37(455-HAT)
S-455-29/45
Secret Ser. 4629

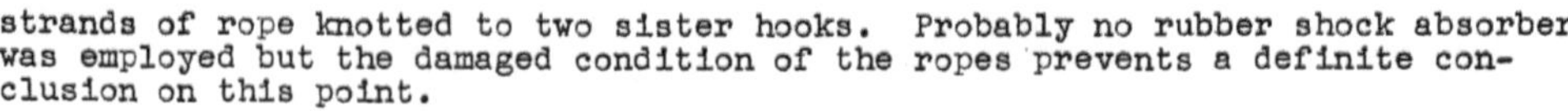

strands of rope knotted to two sister hooks. Probably no rubber shock absorber was employed but the damaged condition of the ropes prevents a definite conclusion on this point.

R. H. BULLARD
Comdr., USNR
By Direction of Director
Naval Research Laboratory

NAVAL RESEARCH LABORATORY

Anacostia Station

Washington, D.C.

S-EF37(455-HAT)

Serial No. 4677
S-455-38/45
as

[redacted]

10 March 1945

DECLASSIFIED

To: Officer in Charge,
Technical Air Intelligence Center,
U. S. Naval Air Station
Anacostia, D. C.

Subj: Balloon, Japanese Paper, from Hayfork, California - CEE No. 22212.

Refs: (a) NRL ltr S-EF37(455-HAT), S-455-8/45 of 15 Jan. 1945 to TAIC.
(b) CG, G-2 Western Defense Command ltr B0211 to G-2, War Department dated 6 Feb. 1945.

1. The subject material was examined at the Naval Air Station, Anacostia on 24 February 1945 by representatives of this Laboratory and certain portions were brought to the Laboratory for further study. The material consisted of the ballast release mechanism and six increments of ballast from a Japanese paper balloon of the type described in reference (a). Reference (b) describes four incendiary bombs which were recovered with this ballast release mechanism. The altitude settings on the barometric contactors (aneroids) as measured at this Laboratory do not agree with the settings reported in reference (b). The hook-up of the contactors was slightly different than that found on previous balloons. A radio type relay was found with this material.

DISCOVERY

2. The subject material is reported to have been recovered at Hayfork, California on 1 February 1945.

INVENTORY

3. The material examined at the Naval Air Station included the ballast release mechanism without battery, six sand filled ballast bags, a Japanese radio type relay, and nine molded rubber rings. According to reference (b) four incendiaries were recovered with or near the release mechanism.

BALLAST RELEASE MECHANISM

4. The ballast release gear was similar to those previously examined. It was suspended on the customary four doubled ropes and evidently no rubber shock absorber had been used.

5. The wood and plastic battery boxes were of the usual size and construction. The battery was not received. A part of the battery connector plug was received.

6. The barometric contactors were mounted in the usual manner but were wired differently. Enclosure (F) of reference (a) shows the customary connections. In this particular case the No. 2 contactor was connected in series with No. 3 and No. 4 which were in parallel. The No. 2 contactor was adjusted to make a contact above a set altitude and to break the contact below that altitude. All other contactors to date have been adjusted to make a contact below a set altitude. This series arrangement [illegible] keep the ballast

DECLASSIFIED

S-EF37(455-HAT)
Serial No. 4677
S-455-38/45
as

release from functioning until the balloon reached the set altitude of No. 2 contactor and might conceivably take the place of the starting fuzes. However, there were starting fuzes with the mechanism. The contactor covers were marked as follows:

#1 - Underlined V in chalk
#2 - Triangle in white paint
#3 - 3 in chalk
#4 - 7 in yellow chalk or crayon

7. The pressure settings of the contactors were as follows:

#1 - Makes contact at 2.2 miles descending and breaks contact at 2.2 miles ascending.
#2 - Breaks contact at 1.5 miles descending and makes contact at 1.6 miles ascending.
#3 - Makes contact at 4.1 miles descending and breaks contact at 4.2 miles ascending.
#4 - Makes contact on a pressure increase of 35 mm of mercury from a minimum. This corresponds to a drop of 0.5 miles starting at 4 miles or 0.7 miles starting at 6.0 miles altitude.

8. All of the blow out plugs above the #24 pair were still in place. In addition to the fuzes from the unfired plugs there were 7 other fuzes which did not burn. None of these were in pairs.

9. Three arming wires were attached to the bottom of the mechanism and a fourth was found in the packing case. Reference (b) describes four incendiary bombs found attached to or near the mechanism when discovered. They were attached in the number 31, 32, 33 and 34 positions.

10. Reference (b) also reports that seven sand bags weighing 4.75 pounds, 4.375 pounds, 2.5 pounds, 2.25 pounds, 2.375 pounds, 2.5 pounds and 6.75 pounds were attached in positions numbered 25, 26, 27, 28, 29, 31 and 35 respectively. The sand in the bags consisted of a mixture of orange-yellow, black and white particles and therefore resembled a mixture of sand from the Marshall and sand from the Holy Cross balloons.

11. The cause of malfunction of the ballast release mechanism could not be ascertained.

12. In the packing case with the material was a Japanese relay which is in effect a four pole double throw solenoid operated switch. A relay identical in appearance but wired slightly differently was found in a Japanese radio transmitter type 99 Hi4 at TAIC. Reference (b) does not mention this item. If it was found with the release mechanism it would indicate that some electronic device had been attached. The electronic device could have been dashed to pieces at some time when the balloon first descended and the relay thrown free and lodged in the release mechanism.

13. Nine molded rubber rings about 5 inches in diameter and having a round 3/32 inch diameter cross section were also found in the packing case. These are not mentioned in reference (b).

R.H. BULLARD
Comdr., USNR
By Direction of Director
Naval Research Laboratory

NAVAL RESEARCH LABORATORY

S-EF37(455-HAT)

Anacostia Station

Washington 2, D. C.

Serial No. 4678
S-455-39/45
as

10 March 1945

To: Officer in Charge
Technical Air Intelligence Center
U. S. Naval Air Station
Anacostia, D. C.

Subj: Balloons, Japanese Paper, from Laurens, Iowa and Schuyler, Nebraska, CEE No. 22201.

Refs: (a) Visit of Lt(jg) C.L. Miller of TAIC to NRL on 12 Feb 1945.
(b) NRL ltr S-EF37(455-HAT) S-455-8/45 of 15 Jan 1945 to TAIC.

1. At the request of the Technical Air Intelligence Center, NAS, Anacostia (reference (a)) the Laboratory has examined the subject balloon parts. The material from Schuyler, Nebraska consisted of a single fragment of paper identical with that used for the envelopes of Japanese paper balloons of the type described in reference (b). The material from Laurens, Iowa consisted of parts of the envelope, the shroud lines, the envelope ignition charge and the envelope ignition charge fuze from the same type of balloon.

DISCOVERY

2. The fragment of paper from Schuyler, Nebraska was discovered on 2 February 1945. The material from Laurens, Iowa was discovered on the same date.

ENVELOPE REMAINS

3. The fragment from Schuyler, Nebraska was a single triangular section about two yards across the base and one yard from base to apex. It appeared to be charred along one edge while the other edges were cut, presumably after discovery. The paper was no different from that used in previous balloons.

4. The material from Laurens, Iowa was in a number of irregular pieces of various sizes. Many appeared to have scorched edges. Possibly the destruction of the balloon by its demolition charge produced the fragmentation and charring. No colored tape was observed on the seams. The skirt was of the usual construction but contained a lighter rope (3/16 inch diameter) than the 1/4 inch rope used on previous balloons. The loops were knotted and bound with hard cord.

SHROUDS

5. The shrouds consisted of the usual 19 branched lines terminating in hooks for attaching to the skirt. The splices and end loops were bound with silk cord. The rope was in new condition.

SUPPORT ROPES

6. The support ropes were knotted through the usual two sister hooks used for attaching to the shrouds. There was no evidence that a rubber shock absorber was used but the condition of the ropes does not permit a definite conclusion on this point. The support ropes consisted of the customary 8 lengths of 3 strand 3/8 inch diameter rope. The lower end terminated in frayed

ends. The rope was weathered in appearance.

ENVELOPE IGNITION CHARGE

7. The envelope ignition charge was the customary cylindrical paper container filled with magnesium flash powder.

ENVELOPE IGNITION CHARGE FUZE

8. There were three sections of fuze totaling approximately 48 feet. This was the same type of fuze found leading to the envelope ignition charge on previous balloons. About one-third of this fuze was burned.

R. H. BULLARD
Comdr., USNR
By Direction of Director
Naval Research Laboratory

NAVAL RESEARCH LABORATORY

S-EF37(455-HAT)

Anacostia Station

Serial No. 4679
S-455-42/45
as

Washington, D.C.

10 March 1945

To: Officer in Charge
Technical Air Intelligence Center
U. S. Naval Air Station
Anacostia, D. C.

Subj: Balloon, Japanese Paper, from Sevastopol, California - CEE No. 22208.

Refs: (a) NRL ltr S-EF37(455-HAT) S-455-8/45 of 15 Jan 1945 to TAIC
(b) NRL ltr S-EF37(455-HAT) S-455-9/45 of 20 Jan 1945 to TAIC

1. The subject material was examined at the Naval Air Station, Anacostia on 24 February 1945 by representatives of this Laboratory and was found to consist of the valve and portions of the envelope and rubber shock absorber from a Japanese paper balloon of the type described in reference (a). Other remains from the same balloon were examined at this Laboratory at an earlier date and described in reference (b).

ENVELOPE

2. The envelope material was identical with that from other balloons of the same type. Blue tape was used on some of the seams. A number of figures, in ink and put on with a rubber stamp, were observed. Apparently the sections of the balloon had been numbered as an aid to assembly.

VALVE

3. The valve was of the type first found on the Estacado balloon and was stamped 4590 on the spring support. There were rope loops on the valve for suspension from the envelope.

SHOCK ABSORBER

4. The shock absorber was of the usual construction consisting of strands of rubber and covered at the two ends with braided cotton and lashed back to form loops.

R. H. BULLARD
Comdr., USNR
By Direction of Director
Naval Research Laboratory

NAVAL RESEARCH LABORATORY

S-EF37(455-HAT)

Anacostia Station

Serial No. 4702
S-455-46/45
as

Washington 20, D. C.

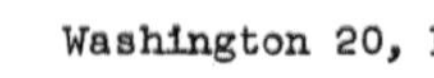

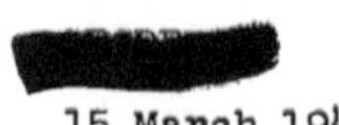

15 March 1945

To: Officer in Charge
Technical Air Intelligence Center
U. S. Naval Air Station
Anacostia, D. C.

Subj: Balloon, Japanese Paper, from Red Bluff, California - CEE No. 22209.

Ref: (a) NRL ltr S-EF37(455-HAT) S-455-8/45 of 15 Jan 1945 to TAIC.

1. The subject material was examined at the Naval Air Station, Anacostia on 24 February 1945 by representatives of this Laboratory and found to consist of the valve and a part of the envelope from a Japanese Paper balloon of the type described in reference (a).

DISCOVERY

2. Recovery was at Red Bluff, California on 2 February 1945.

ENVELOPE

3. The material examined consisted of approximately one-fourth of an envelope and was from the lower half. It was identical in composition and construction with other balloons of this type. Blue tape had been used for patching material at some places.

VALVE

4. The valve was of the type first found on the Kalispell balloon. It was numbered 7100 in white paint on the valve disc. There were no rope loops for suspension from the envelope. The rubber seal differed from any other valve to date in that it was black whereas the others have been natural.

R. H. BULLARD
Comdr., USNR
By Direction of Director
Naval Research Laboratory

NAVAL RESEARCH LABORATORY

S-EF(455-LBL)Ser. 4[illegible]0 Anacostia Station

S-455-33/45 Washington 20, D.C.
map

21 March 1945

To: Officer in Charge
Technical Air Intelligence Center
U. S. Naval Air Station
Anacostia, D. C.

Subj: Balloon, Japanese Paper, from Newcastle, Wyoming - CEE 22122.

Refs: (a) Visit to TAIC, NAS, Anacostia following telephone conversation of Lt(jg) C.L. Miller of TAIC with Lt. H.A. Tanner of NRL, 16 Feb 1945.
(b) NRL ltr S-EF37(455-HAT), S-455-8/45 of 15 Jan 1945 to TAIC.
(c) NRL ltr S-EF37(455-HAT), S-455-30/45 of 23 Feb 1945 to TAIC.

1. At the request of the Technical Air Intelligence Center, NAS, Anacostia (Reference (a)), the Laboratory has examined the subject balloon at the Naval Air Station, Anacostia. It was found to consist of the envelope, valve, shroud lines, and remains of the ballast release mechanism similar to those previously described (Reference (b)). This examination has supplied no new information in regard to the origin, operation or purpose of these balloons.

DISCOVERY

2. The balloon was discovered at Newcastle, Wyoming on 8 February 1945.

INVENTORY

3. The material examined at the Naval Air Station, Anacostia, consisted of the envelope, shroud lines, valve, remains of the metal framework of the ballast release mechanism, starter fuzes and an electrical connector.

ENVELOPE

4. The envelope was similar in size, shape and general construction to the other paper envelopes previously described. The paper segments were fastened together with both brown and blue-green tape with brown predominating. The rope in the skirt was 3-ply 1/4 inch diameter rope. There were six small rope loops near the bottom of the envelope but they were not attached to the valve. There was no evidence that an incendiary charge had been attached to the envelope.

5. Inside the balloon, two to three feet from the crown, several numbers were found: "03" and "14" written in pencil, "70" (several of these) stenciled in one-inch blue numerals, and "4", "5" and "5" written on the under surface of the tape used to cover the seams between several of the paper segments.

VALVE

6. The relief valve was similar to those of the Kalispell, Holy Cross and Alturas balloons. A photograph and discussion of the types of valves may be found in Reference (c). The valve had on it the numbers "9060" in white paint and "12" or "112" in chalk. There were six small rope loops located around the circumference of the valve seat but they were not used.

S-EF37(455-LBL) Ser. 4640
S-455-33/45
map

SHROUD LINES

7. The ropes were of the usual number (19 3-ply 3/8-inch diameter lines) and arrangement, and were in good condition. They were fastened at the bottom to the usual triangular iron ring.

SNUBBER

8. There was no rubber shock absorber (snubber) found with the balloon.

BALLAST RELEASE MECHANISM

9. Only the remains of the metal framework consisting of four iron posts, angle iron braces, and pieces of bakelite were found. The usual starter fuzes were wrapped around the framework. A bakelite electrical connector was found unattached to any of the other material. There was no evidence that the ballast release mechanism differed from others previously described.

R. H. BULLARD
Comdr., USNR
By Direction of Director
Naval Research Laboratory

NAVAL RESEARCH LABORATORY

S-EF37(455:HAT)Ser.4758

S-455-57/45
pmp

Anacostia Station

Washington, D. C.

28 March 1945

To: Officer in Charge
Technical Air Intelligence Center
U. S. Naval Air Station
Anacostia, D. C.

Subj: Balloon, Japanese Paper, from Glendo, Wyoming, CEE No. 22223.

Ref: (a) NRL ltr S-EF37(455:HAT), S-455-8/45 of 15 Jan 1945 to TAIC.

1. The subject material has been examined by representatives of the Laboratory at the request of TAIC. The material consisted of the envelope, shrouds, valve, ballast release mechanism, and one unit of ballast from a Japanese paper balloon of the type described in Ref. (a). There were no important differences between this and earlier balloons of the same type. The envelope material was the four ply type found in several recent balloons.

SOURCE

2. This balloon was observed grounding near Glendo, Wyoming on 22 February 1945.

ENVELOPE

3. The envelope was of the usual size, shape, and general construction. No colored tape was used on the envelope except for some small patches of greenish blue colored tape covering flaws in the paper. The sections were numbered with two inch purple stamped figures. The number 124 was stamped on the apex in 7/8 inch figures. There was a paper cylinder attached for insertion of an ignition charge but it had not been used. Only four layers could be detected in the paper envelope material.

VALVE

4. The valve was of the type first found on the Estacado balloon. The number 4895 was stamped on the spring seat and written in chalk on the valve. There were no rope loops on the valve.

SHROUDS

5. The shrouds were identical with those from previous balloons. The hooks used for attaching the shrouds to the envelope were of a slightly different shape than those found on earlier balloons.

BALLAST RELEASE MECHANISM

6. The battery, barometric contactors, and demolition charge were missing from the release mechanism. Suspension was by the usual ropes and no rubber shock absorber had been used. White triangles were painted on two sides of the battery box and the usual starting fuzes were wrapped around this box.

7. All of the blow out or ballast release plugs above and including the No. 26 pair were unfired and carried the usual "Tees" for the attachment of ballast and incendaries. The No. 27, No. 28, and No. 29 Tees carried light ropes corresponding to the small ballast bags, the No. 32 Tee carried ropes corresponding to a large ballast bag. On the other unfired plugs including the two

S-EF37(455:HAT)Ser.4758
S-455-57/45
pmp

DECLASSIFIED

center plugs there were empty tees of nothing at all. Both center plugs were out of position. One had a short length of unfired fuze attached and the other had attached a two foot length of fuze terminating in a detonator which explodes the demolition charge. There were four instances where isolated fuzes had failed to ignite. The reason for the balloon grounding before the ballast was exhausted could not be ascertained but may have been a defective battery.

8. Two arming wires were attached, one at the #35 release plugs and one near the center release plugs.

9. The ballast bag was one of the larger type sand filled paper bags and weighed six pounds as received. The sand was similar in general appearance to that from the Hayfork balloon but was of smaller particle size.

R. H. BULLARD
Comdr., USNR
By Direction of Director
Naval Research Laboratory

NAVAL RESEARCH LABORATORY

S-EF37(455:HAT)

Anacostia Station

S-455-58/45
Secret Ser. #4753
kos

Washington 20, D. C.

[redacted]

30 March 1945

DECLASSIFIED

To: Officer in Charge
Technical Air Intelligence Center
U. S. Naval Air Station
Anacostia, D. C.

Subj: Balloon, Japanese Paper, from Powell, Wyoming, CEE No. 22225.

Ref: (a) NRL ltr S-EF37(455-HAT), S-455-8/45 of 15 Jan 1945 to TAIC.

1. The subject material was examined at the Naval Air Station, Anacostia, by representatives of the Laboratory at the request of TAIC. The material was found to consist of the valve and a fragment of the envelope from a Japanese paper balloon of the type described in Reference (a). The paper envelope was made from four ply laminated paper of the type found in several recent balloons.

SOURCE

2. The subject balloon was observed exploding in the air near Powell, Wyoming on 22 February 1945. In addition to the valve and envelope fragment it is reported that three thermite bombs and the remains of a large (25 pound) bomb of undetermined type were recovered.

ENVELOPE FRAGMENT

3. The envelope fragment was attached to the valve and was a segment extending upwards 13 feet from the valve and approximately 20 feet wide at the upper end. The material was laminated paper of the four layer type. No colored tape was in evidence.

VALVE

4. The valve was of the type first found on the Kalispell balloon and was numbered 3468 in white paint. The number 14 was written on in chalk in two places. There were rope loops for suspending the valve from the envelope but they were not used.

R. H. BULLARD
Comdr., USNR
By Direction of Director
Naval Research Laboratory

NAVAL RESEARCH LABORATORY

S-EF37(455:LBL) Ser. 4743 Anacostia Station

S-455-52/45 Washington, D. C.
pmp

28 March 1945

To: Officer in Charge,
Technical Air Intelligence Center,
U. S. Naval Air Station,
Anacostia, D. C.

Subj: Balloon, Japanese, from Prosser, Wash., CEE 22220.

Ref: (a) Visit to NAS, Anacostia, following telephone conversation of 9 March 1945 of Lt(jg) C.L. Miller of TAIC, USNAS, Anacostia with Lt. H.A. Tanner of NRL.
(b) NRL ltr S-EF37(455:HAT) S-455-8/45 of 15 Jan 1945 to TAIC.

1. At the request of TAIC (reference (a)), an examination was made of parts of the balloon found at Prosser, Washington. The material examined was similar in design and function to the corresponding parts of previous balloons, (reference (b)). No reason for the failure of the balloon to destroy itself was apparent from the material examined. It may be surmised that the production of these balloons has become more or less routine since only a few numbers were stamped on the ballast ring as guides in assembly.

DISCOVERY

2. The balloon was found near Prosser, Wash., on 13 February 1945.

INVENTORY

3. The material examined consisted of the ballast release mechanism and the aneroids. The envelope and valve were reported to have been found also but had not been received at the time this examination was made.

ANEROIDS

4. The aneroids were in very good condition. The altitude settings were determined and should be reliable if the adjusting screws have not been turned since the discovery.

#1 - "8" in chalk on cover. Setting: makes contact below 0.6 miles.
#2 - " " in white paint on cover. Setting: makes contact above 1.2 miles.
#3 - Setting: makes contact below 4.25 miles.
#4 - Double bellows in center. Makes contact after a pressure increase of 36 mm. corresponding to a decrease in altitude of about 0.6 miles at a height of 5 miles.

BALLAST RELEASE MECHANISM

5. The ballast release mechanism was of the usual type and was supported in the usual manner by 3-ply 3/8" diameter ropes. The storage battery was missing. There was no evidence that a rubber shock absorber (snubber) had been used. The usual starter fuses were present.

6. The bakelite portion of the ballast release mechanism was broken in several places. The usual painted numbers (1 through 36) were missing from

this insulation, and also only a few numbers (10) were stamped onto the ballast ring. This would indicate that the process of assembly has become routine, and that only a few numbers are necessary to serve as guides. As far as could be discovered, the electrical hook-up was the same as that of the previously discovered gear.

7. Two unfired plugs and one unfired trigger switch were found but were not situated so as to interfere with the release of ballast. Both center plugs had been fired and the fuse leading from one of them had been ignited. This fuse was broken off a short distance from the center plug. The other fuse was completely gone. Five arming wires of the usual type were tied to the ballast ring.

R. H. BULLARD
Comdr., USNR
By Direction of Director
Naval Research Laboratory

NAVAL RESEARCH LABORATORY

S-EF37(455:LBL)Ser. 4742 Anacostia Station

S-455-51/45 Washington, D. C.
pmp

29 March 1945

DECLASSIFIED

To: Officer in Charge
Technical Air Intelligence Center
U. S. Naval Air Station
Anacostia, D. C.

Subj: Balloon, Japanese, from Tremonton, Utah, CEE #22219.

Ref: (a) Visit to Naval Air Station, Anacostia, following telephone conversation of 9 March 1945 of Lt(jg) C.L. Miller of TAIC, USNAS, Anacostia with Lt. H.A. Tanner of NRL.
(b) NRL ltr S-EF37(455:HAT) S-455-8/45 of 15 January 1945 to TAIC.

1. At the request of the Technical Air Intelligence Center (reference (a)), an examination was made of parts of the balloon found at Tremonton, Utah. The material examined was similar in design and function to corresponding parts of balloons previously examined (reference (b)). Failure of the fuse leading to some destruction device (not found) probably accounts for the lack of destruction of the balloon.

DISCOVERY

2. The balloon was found near Tremonton, Utah, on 23 February 1945.

INVENTORY

3. The material examined consisted of the ballast release mechanism including the ballast ring, aneroids, battery and anti-freeze solution and the supporting ropes. The envelope and valve were reported to have been found but had not been received at the time this examination was made.

ANEROIDS

4. The aneroids were not in good condition and their protective covers were missing. The settings of the aneroids were determined but are not reliable due to the poor condition of the equipment and to the possibility that the adjusting screws had been turned.

#1 - "4000" written in pencil on aluminum base. Chalk character on bottom of base. Setting: makes contact below 1.2 miles.
#2 - "2200" in pencil on base. Setting: makes contact above 0.6 miles.
#3 - "?800" in pencil on base. Setting: makes contact below 4.25 miles.
#4 - Double bellows in center. Makes contact after a pressure increase of 34 mm. corresponding to a decrease in altitude of about 0.6 miles at an altitude of 5 miles.

BATTERY

5. The battery housing consisting of the celluloid boxes, anti-freeze solution, and the storage battery was found intact. It had, however, been disconnected from the remainder of the ballast release mechanism.

DECLASSIFIED

S-EF37(455:LBL)Ser. 4742
S-455-51/45
pmp

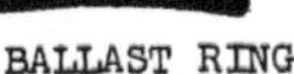

BALLAST RING

6. The ballast release mechanism was of the usual type and was supported by the usual arrangement of 3-ply, 3/8" diameter ropes. There was no evidence of a rubber shock absorber (snubber) having been used. The usual starter fuses were present.

7. Three unfired trigger switches and one unfired plug were found but these were not located so as to break the chain of firing or to prevent any ballast from having been released. Both center plugs had been fired but only one fuse had been ignited. Both fuses were very short - the fired fuse had been cut off about 2 inches from the plug and the unfired one cut off about 24 inches from the center plug. This longer fuse was probably the one that should have led to the destruction of the balloon.

8. There were five arming wires present---one tied near the center of the ring, two tied through the holes where the #36 plugs should have been, and two on the opposite side of the ring.

R. H. BULLARD
Comdr., USNR
By Direction of Director
Naval Research Laboratory

NAVAL RESEARCH LABORATORY

S-EF37(455:HAT) Ser. 4749 Anacostia Station

S-455-54/45 Washington, D. C.
pmp

29 March 1945

To: Officer in Charge
Technical Air Intelligence Center
U. S. Naval Air Station
Anacostia, D. C.

Subj: Balloon, Japanese paper, from Grand Rapids, Michigan, CEE No. 22216.

Ref: (a) NRL ltr S-EF37(455:HAT), S-455-8/45 of 15 Jan 1945 to TAIC.

1. At the request of TAIC, representatives of the Laboratory have examined the subject balloon materials at the Naval Air Station, Anacostia. The material was identified as the envelope, valve, and shrouds from a Japanese paper balloon of the type described in reference (a). There was also one metal hook of the type which has been used to suspend incendiaries from these balloons. These components did not differ from those of other balloons of this type except that the envelope material apparently consisted of four laminated layers in place of the usual five. The shroud line hooks were also slightly different in shape.

DISCOVERY

2. This material is reported to have been recovered at Grand Rapids, Michigan on 23 February 1945.

ENVELOPE

3. The envelope was one of the usual size and design. The material was identical in appearance but only four laminated layers could be detected. The patches used over flaws in the material seemed somewhat larger than normal. The seams were covered mainly with white tape but some blue tape was also used. No evidence of an envelope ignition charge was observed. The sections were numbered with 1 inch and 2 inch stamped figures.

VALVE

4. The valve was of the type first found on the Estacado balloon. The number 6028 was stamped on the spring seat and written in chalk on the valve. There were no rope loops of the type sometimes used for suspending the valve from the bag.

SHROUDS

5. The shrouds were in new condition and were of the usual size and arrangement. The hooks used to attach the shrouds to the envelope were somewhat different in shape than those observed on previous balloons.

R. H. BULLARD
Comdr., USNR
By Direction of Director
Naval Research Laboratory

NAVAL RESEARCH LABORATORY

S-EF37(455-HAT) Ser. 4741 Anacostia Station

S-455-53/45 Washington 20, D. C.
pmp

29 March 1945

To: Officer in Charge
Technical Air Intelligence Center
U. S. Naval Air Station
Anacostia, D. C.

Subj: Balloons, Japanese Paper Envelope Fragments from Ontario, Oregon (C.E.E. No. 22207) and Flathead Bay, Montana (C.E.E. No. 22222).

Ref: (a) NRL ltr S-EF37(455-HAT) S-455-8/45 of 15 Jan 1945 to TAIC.

1. The subject balloon envelope fragments have been examined by the Laboratory at the request of TAIC. In both cases, the material has been identified as parts from the envelopes of Japanese paper balloons of the type described in reference (a). The paper from Ontario, Oregon differs from previous balloons in that only four layers of paper were cemented together instead of the usual five layers. The paper from Flathead Bay, Montana consisted of the usual five layers but had been improperly manufactured or had weathered extensively causing separation into two layers over a considerable portion of the surface.

2. The Ontario, Oregon material was discovered on 2 Feb 1945. The fragment received at the Laboratory was about two feet square. There was no colored tape in evidence. The thickness of the paper was around .005 inches whereas in previous cases, the thickness has ranged from .0065 to .0090 inches. Only four layers could be detected. The paper was otherwise the same as that from the other balloons of this type.

3. The Flathead Bay, Montana material consisted of around fifty square feet in one piece and apparently was from the upper portion of the envelope. The seams were covered with blue tape. Some of the segments were numbered with stamped numerals and letters. The paper was separated into two layers at a number of places, evidently due to faulty manufacture. Five layers were detected in the paper and it was a little lighter in weight and color compared to the earlier balloons. Probably the amount of cementing material used was less than before or had been washed out by extensive weathering.

R. H. BULLARD
Comdr., USNR
By Direction of Director
Naval Research Laboratory

NAVAL RESEARCH LABORATORY

S-EF37(455:HAT)Ser.4750
455-55/45
pmp

Anacostia Station
Washington, D. C.

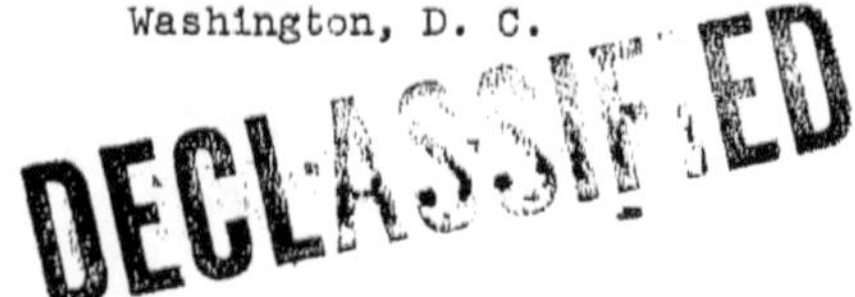

29 March 1945

To: Officer in Charge
Technical Air Intelligence Center
U. S. Naval Air Station
Anacostia, D. C.

Subj: Balloon, Japanese Paper, from Camp Beale, Marysville, California, CEE No. 22217.

Ref: (a) NRL ltr S-EF37(455:HAT), S-455-8/45 of 15 Jan 1945 to TAIC.

1. The subject material has been examined at the Naval Air Station, Anacostia at the request of TAIC by representatives of the Laboratory. The material consisted of the valve and the ballast release mechanism (less battery and barometric contactors) from a Japanese paper balloon of the type described in reference (a). There were no significant differences between these components and those from other balloons of this type.

DISCOVERY

2. This balloon grounded at Camp Beale, Marysville, California on 8 February 1945.

VALVE

3. The valve was of the type first found on the Kalispell balloon and bore the number 13420 in white paint. There were no rope loops for suspension of the valve from the envelope.

BALLAST RELEASE MECHANISM

4. The ballast release mechanism was suspended on ropes in the customary manner. No rubber shock absorber had been used. The usual starting fuzes were present. There were two arming wires tied on near the #35 ballast release plugs, two near the #36 plugs, and one at the center of the ballast ring.

5. All the release plugs above and including the #20 pair were unfired. The two center plugs also were unfired. There was no "Tee" on the center plugs but all the other pairs of plugs carried "Tees". The #20, #23, and #26 Tees had heavy cord strings attached which would correspond to the six pound size ballast bags. The #22, #28, and #29 Tees had light strings attached corresponding to the smaller ballast bags which usually weigh about 2.5 pounds. The #24 and #30 Tees had heavy ropes attached suggesting that they carried incendiaries. The #33 Tee had attached to it a wire hook identical with that found on one of the Medford incendiaries. One #19 and one #21 plug were unfired. The other #21 plug was missing and the other #19 plug fired but the fuze failed to ignite. As a result, the #20 switches did not close preventing the release of any further ballast units. The cause of failure of the center plug fuzed to the demolition charge to function could not be ascertained. This fuze was about two feet long and terminated in a cut end. Presumably a demolition charge was removed from this before shipment. The fuze from the other center plug was cut off at the plug.

R. H. BULLARD
Comdr., USNR
By Direction of Director
Naval Research Laboratory

NAVAL RESEARCH LABORATORY

S-EF37(455-HAT) Anacostia Station

S-455-59/45 Washington 20, D. C.
Secret Ser. #4754
kos

30 March 1945

To: Officer in Charge
Technical Air Intelligence Center
U. S. Naval Air Station
Anacostia, D. C.

Subj: Balloon, Japanese Paper, from Kirby, Wyoming, CEE No. 22224.

Ref: (a) NRL ltr S-EF37(455-HAT), S-455-8/45 of 15 Jan 1945 to TAIC.

1. The subject material has been examined by representatives of the Laboratory at the request of TAIC. The material consisted of the ballast release mechanism from a Japanese paper balloon of the type described in Reference (a). It did not differ appreciably from those on previous balloons.

SOURCE.

2. This balloon was observed grounding at Kirby, Wyoming on 22 February 1945. In addition to the ballast release mechanism it is reported that the envelope, valve, and shrouds were recovered.

BALLAST RELEASE MECHANISM.

3. Suspension of the release mechanism was on ropes of the usual type and no rubber shock absorber was used. The battery was in a discharged condition and the inner plastic box which ordinarily is filled with a calcium chloride solution was cracked open at the bottom and was empty. The metal container for the demolition charge was still in place beside the battery. The usual starting fuzes were wrapped around the battery box.

4. The barometric contactors were of the usual type. The No. 2 contactor was adjusted to make a contact ascending and was connected in series with No. 3 and No. 4 which were in parallel. There were white triangles painted on two sides of the battery box. It has been observed that when these triangles are present the No. 2 contactor is hooked up as above. Similar markings on the contactor covers and the same hook-up were found on the Hayfork and Prosser balloons.

5. The altitude settings of the contactors were as follows:

#1 - Makes contact descending and breaks contact ascending at 1.87 miles altitude.
#2 - Makes contact ascending and breaks contact descending at 1.84 miles altitude.
#3 - Makes contact descending at 3.15 miles and breaks contact ascending at 3.86 miles. Contacts were corroded.
#4 - Makes contact on pressure increase of 42 mm. mercury at 500 mm. This corresponds to a drop of 0.6 miles at 5.0 miles altitude.

6. The markings on the contactors were as follows:

#1 - No cover and no marking.
#2 - No cover. Number 700 in pencil on base.
#3 - No cover. Number 7800 in pencil on base.
#4 - White chalk triangel on cover.

S-EF37(455-HAT)
S-455-59/45
Secret Ser. No. 4754

7. Apparently the balloon exhausted the supply of ballast and ignited one of the two center fuzes, which terminated in a burned end. It was not possible to determine whether this fuze had lead to the demolition charge or to an envelope ignition charge. The other center fuze was missing. There was one unfired plug not in position, one fired plug still in position, and two isolated unfired fuzes connecting blowout plugs with trigger switches. The reason for failure of the demolition charge to explode could not be determined.

8. There were four short and one long arming wires attached below the release mechanism.

R. H. BULLARD
Commander, USNR
By Direction of Director
Naval Research Laboratory

NAVAL RESEARCH LABORATORY

S-EF37(455-HAT)

Anacostia Station

Ser. No. 4792
S-455-60/45
as

Washington 20, D. C.

30 March 1945

DECLASSIFIED

To: Officer in Charge
Technical Air Intelligence Center
U. S. Naval Air Station
Anacostia, D. C.

Subj: Balloon, Japanese Paper, from Julian, California - CEE #22210.

Ref: (a) NRL ltr S-EF37(455-HAT) S-455-8/45 of 15 Jan 1945 to TAIC.

1. At the request of TAIC the Laboratory has examined the subject balloon remains and identified them as the relief valve and ballast release mechanism from a Japanese paper balloon of the type described in ref. (a). No significant differences were noticed between these items and the corresponding parts of earlier balloons of this type.

DISCOVERY

2. The subject material was discovered near Julian, California on 1 February 1945. In addition to the relief valve and ballast release mechanism the envelope shrouds, envelope ignition charge and demolition charge were recovered.

VALVE

3. The valve was of the type first found on the Kalispell balloon and bore the number 11318 in white paint.

BALLAST RELEASE MECHANISM

4. The ballast release mechanism was supported on ropes knotted to two sister hooks. There was no evidence that a rubber shock absorber had been used.

5. The release gear was identical with those previously examined. There were the two usual starting fuzes and also a long fuze of the type used to connect the release mechanism with the envelope incendiary. The long fuze was burned part way through. A failure in this fuze prevented destruction of the envelope which is reported to have been recovered but has not been received at TAIC.

6. All of the blow out plugs above and including the No. 33 pair were unfired. One No. 31 plug was unfired and there were 6 isolated cases where fuzes connecting blow out plugs and switches had failed to ignite. Due to the damaged and dismantled condition of the mechanism the cause of failure could not be established but may have been due to a battery failure or to some mistake in assembly. The latter is more probable as this would explain why the long fuze to the envelope ignitor had been lighted but the fuze leading to the demolition charge had not been ignited. With the customary wiring the long fuze to the envelope cannot ignite until all of the pairs of ballast release plugs have fired and the demolition charge fuze is ignited at any time if the balloon descends below the altitude set on the #1 barometric contactor.

S-EF37(455-HAT)
Ser. No. 4792
S-455-60/45
as

7. The altitude settings on the barometric contactors were:

#1 - Made contact below 4.1 miles
#2 - Made contact below 4.3 miles
#3 - Made contact below 5.2 miles
#4 - Made contact on a pressure increase of 55 mm. of mercury corresponding to a descent of 0.6 miles at 5.0 miles altitude. The setting on the #1 contactor is for a higher altitude than usual.

8. The barometric contactors were marked as follows:

#1 - "4000" in pencil on base, "30" in chalk beneath
#2 - "7760" in pencil on the base
#3 - "8" in chalk on bottom
#4 - "700" in pencil on the base

9. There were five instances where individual fuzes from blow out plugs to switches failed to ignite. None of these were in pairs. These are in addition to the unburned fuzes from the unfired plugs.

10. No incendiaries or ballast units were recovered. The #35 pair of blow out plugs carried a "Tee" to which was attached a length of rope and a hook corresponding to the usual method for attaching an incendiary.

R. H. BULLARD
Comdr., USNR
By Direction of Director
Naval Research Laboratory

NAVAL RESEARCH LABORATORY

S-EF37(455-HAT)

Anacostia Station

Serial No. 4793
S-455-61/45
as

Washington 20, D. C.

31 March 1945

To: Officer in Charge
Technical Air Intelligence Center
U. S. Naval Air Station
Anacostia, D. C.

Subj: Balloon, Japanese Paper, from Burwell, Nebraska - CEE No. 22215.

Refs: (a) NRL ltr S-EF37(455-HAT) S-455-8/45 of 15 Jan 1945 to TAIC
(b) NRL ltr S-EF37(455-HAT) S-455-38/45 of 10 Mar 1945 to TAIC

1. At the request of TAIC the subject material has been examined at the Naval Air Station, Anacostia and was found to consist of the envelope, shrouds, valve and ballast release mechanism from a Japanese paper balloon of the type described in reference (a). No significant differences between this and other balloons of the same type were observed.

DISCOVERY

2. The subject material is reported to have been discovered at Burwell, Nebraska on 12 February 1945.

ENVELOPE

3. The envelope was of the usual size, shape and general appearance. The seams were covered mainly with white tape but some blue-green tape had been used. The material of the envelope consisted of the usual five cemented layers. The sections of the envelope were numbered with 3/4" red stamped figures. There was an unused paper cylinder cemented to the envelope. This is for an envelope ignition charge when one is used.

VALVE

4. The valve was of the type first found on the Estacado balloon but had the number 6697 in green paint. In previous valves of this type the number has been stamped into the metal. There were rope loops on the valve for attachment to the envelope.

SHROUDS

5. The shrouds were identical with those from previous balloons and were in new condition.

BALLAST RELEASE MECHANISM

6. No battery and no barometric contactors were with the ballast release mechanism. The usual starting fuzes were wrapped around the battery box. All of the ballast release plugs above and including the #30 pair were unfired. There were two other unfired plugs and three other cases where fuzes leading from fired plugs did not ignite. Only one of the center release plugs remained in position. This was unfired and was connected to a fuze which terminated in a cut end.

7. There were two arming wires tied on near the #35 release plugs, two tied on near the #36 release plugs and one tied to the bottom center of the apparatus.

S-EF37(455-HAT)
Ser. No. 4793
S-455-61/45
as

8. The battery box had a white triangle painted on two opposite sides. There is some reason for believing that a white triangle signifies that barometric contactors are arranged like those in the Hayfork balloon (ref. (b)) with one of the contactors of the ballast releasing group in series with the other two and adjusted to break contact below a set altitude.

9. The cause of the failure of the balloon to exhause the ballast could not be ascertained. Possibly there was a failure of the battery from some cause.

R. H. BULLARD
Comdr., USNR
By Direction of Director
Naval Research Laboratory

NAVAL RESEARCH LABORATORY

S-S67-5/RCM(379)
Serial 4590
1f

Anacostia Station

Washington 20, D.C.

DECLASSIFIED

20 February 1945

To: Commander-in-Chief, U.S. Fleet,
Att: Code F47.

Subj: Radar - Tests of Radar-Visibility of the Metallic Structure of the Japanese Transpacific Balloon.

Ref: (a) BuShips Secret ltr S-S67-5(924-4), S-920-4503 to NRL, dated 11 May 1943.
(b) NRL Secret Report R-2232, dated 18 February 1944: "Radar Cross Section of Ship Targets, II".

1. The radar-visibility tests of the metallic structure of the Japanese transpacific balloons were made to determine at what ranges it would be possible to detect these balloons in flight, with either shore-based or airborne radar, and to determine further which radar frequencies are best for effecting such detection. Because of work done at this laboratory on development of balloon-borne radar reflectors for deception purposes, as requested in the letter of reference (a) (NRL Problem S22R-S), the equipment and techniques for performing these radarvisibility tests were available. The tests were performed at the NRL Chesapeake Bay Annex on 14 through 16 February 1945. Radar equipment on frequencies of from 100 Mc to 10,000 Mc was used. Results indicate maximum radar-visibility at about 200 Mc, with a probable maximum detection range of about 25 nautical miles at this frequency.

2. The metallic structures tested were light-weight simulations of those attached to the Japanese balloons made available at the Chemistry Division of this laboratory. These metallic parts were: (a) a gas valve, and (b) a ballast-control device. The ballast material was sand (a large number of approximately five pound bags was used). It is believed that these would not give an appreciable radar echo. In shape the gas valve roughly resembled an ash-can cover of about 19½-inch diameter, with a 4-inch vertical skirt. Surmounting the valve was a sort of bent-over tripod structure of metal straps about 1½ inches wide, with its feet resting on the perimeter of the valve structure and the legs extending straight up for about 5 inches, then bending over to meet above the center of the valve. At this juncture a coiled spring was attached; this spring connected to the center part of the valve, holding it closed against the pressure of the gas inside the balloon. The ballast-control device consisted mainly of two heavy metal rings spaced about one inch apart, one above the other. The diameter of the rings was about two feet. Interlaced around the inside circumference of the upper ring was some cabled wiring (small-sized insulated wire). Above the center of the rings was a light wood housing which contained batteries and barometric switches. There was a metal framework associated with this housing, with overall dimensions of about one foot (height) by ten inches by ten inches. All metallic parts were duplicated in approximate size and shape. Aluminum foil supported by cardboard was used where possible, for lightness. Aluminum tubing was used where greater strength was needed. The two metallic parts were suspended beneath a Navy Type ZKM balloon for the first series of tests, with the simulated units about 15 feet apart, the gas valve above and the ballast device below. After the first tests, these structures were suspended below a 350-gram aerological balloon and set free. Finally, the ZKM Balloon was observed by itself.

3. On 14 February the simulated metallic structures were suspended beneath a ZKM balloon and flown from a small power boat for radar observations. The propagation path was entirely over water (Chesapeake Bay). The altitudes

of flight were chosen so that the targets being tested would be in or near a maximum in the surface-interference radiation pattern for each radar equipment; i.e., during the measurements with each radar equipment, the height of the target was adjusted for maximum reading. Measurements were made for two ranges: approximately 4000 yards and approximately 8000 yards. The relative power levels of the radar-receiver minimum detectable signal and of the balloon-borne target were measured, utilizing the pulsed-signal-generator technique and equipment developed originally for the measurement of ship-target radar cross section, as described in the report of reference (b). From the data thus obtained the maximum radar-detection range was calculated by computing the range for which the power level for the target echo would be equal to the power level of the minimum detectable signal.

4. On 15 February the target being tested was suspended beneath a 350 gram aerological balloon and released. The free lift of the balloon with reflector attached was such that, with the wind which existed at that time, an altitude of about 17,000 feet was attained at 12 miles range. The altitude beyond this range was not determined. The maximum range was determined by observation with several of the shore-installed radars used in the preceding day's tests. Airborne ASD and ASB were also used. The SCR717C (similar to Navy ASG) provided by the Army for these tests became inoperative shortly after the take-off and could not be used. No echo was observed with the ASB. Range data for the ASD and for the various shore-based radars appears in the following table.

5. In the following table, Range A is the maximum range in free space estimated from the calculated maximum range in the surface interference pattern (calculation made from data obtained as described in paragraph 3). Range B is the maximum range calculated from the data obtained as described in paragraph 3, with the target assumed to be in the interference-pattern maximum. Range C is the maximum range observed on the "free" target as it was wind-borne away from the station (see paragraph 4). Range D is the range at which the measurements described in paragraph 3 were made.

Radar	Frequency	Range A	Range B	Range C	Range D
SCR270	106 Mc	30 miles	58 miles	20 miles	3000 yards
SCR270		21 miles	42 miles	----	8000 yards
SC-2	200 Mc	23 miles	47 miles	24 miles	7800 yards
SC-2		19 miles	38 miles	----	3400 yards
Mark 4	700 Mc	4½ miles	9 miles	4 miles	7300 yards
Mark 4		3½ miles	7½ miles	----	2500 yards
Mark 12	950 Mc	3 miles	6 miles	----	2800 yards
SG	3000 Mc	----	4 miles	----	5120 yards
SP	3000 Mc	----	----	12 miles	----
ASD	10,000 Mc	----	----	2 miles	----

Ranges A, B, and C as given above are in nautical miles. The shore-installed radar antennas were between 115 and 135 feet above the water.

6. Measurements made on the ZKM balloon alone indicate that at the lower frequencies it contributed so little to the equivalent reflecting area that it can be neglected. Only in the S-band was the balloon's radar cross section great enough to make an appreciable difference. It is apparent from the test results that the metallic parts have resonant properties for the

S-S67-5/RCM(379)
Serial 4590
lf

lower frequencies, and that at the higher frequencies (S-band) the gas bag makes a substantial contribution to the radar cross section. Because the motor launch, from which the balloon and target were towed, also gave an appreciable echo at S-band, the measurements of echo returned from the ZKM balloon alone were made with it anchored to a rowboat, to eliminate echo from the boat as much as possible. (At lower frequencies there was no measurable echo from either the boat or the balloon alone.) Because of measurement difficulties, some hint of which may be obtained from the foregoing discussion, an exact statement of the reflecting properties of the ZKM balloon cannot be made. It can, however, be stated that at S-band the echo from the balloon is comparable to that from the metallic structure being tested. Because of the comparatively large radar cross section of the balloon, the data obtained on the SG are inaccurate, but give a qualitative measure of its effectiveness compared to the lower frequency equipment. However, since a small aerological balloon was used to obtain the data listed under "Range C" (paragraph 5), no correction for the balloon was necessary in the case of the data obtained with the SP radar.

7. The maximum ranges obtained (column C) are considerably less than the calculated ranges (column B) because the calculation made use of data taken in the maximum of a surface-interference lobe. During the tests with the free balloon, it was not possible to determine at all times the altitude of the target. Therefore it is not known whether, at the maximum ranges observed, the target was near a maximum or a null of the interference pattern. This statement is not applicable, however, to the data obtained during this test with the SP radar, since at the elevation angles observed the SP antenna beam is sufficiently narrow in the vertical plane so that there is no surface-reflected ray. Therefore, the SP maximum range figure listed under "Range C" in paragraph 5 is the "free space" maximum range.

8. The tests at the Chesapeake Bay Annex were observed by an engineer from the U.S. Army Camp Evans Signal Laboratory. In the near future the Signal Corps plans to conduct radar-visibility tests of one of the actual Japanese gas bags (which are much larger than the U.S. Navy ZKM balloon). It is understood that the SCR-584 and SCR-545 radars will be used. It is planned to have an engineer from the Naval Research Laboratory observe these tests.

9. It should be pointed out that the tests reported here were made on simulations of the metallic parts found on Japanese balloons recovered to date. It is thought to be quite probable that some further object, possibly made of metal, is normally suspended from these balloons, and that no samples of this "object" have yet been recovered (the "object" may be, for example, a bomb or other device which is self-destructive). If this should be found to be the case, the radar detection ranges reported here would obviously be proved inapplicable, since such an object would be quite likely to have a greater radar cross section than the metallic parts already tested.

Distribution:
Cominch, US Fleet, Copy #1
BuShips, Code 920, Copy #2
CNO, Op-25-A2, Copy #3
CNO, OP-26-S, Copy #4
MarCorps, Copy #5
BuAer, Aer-E-3143, Copy #6
CNO, Op-16-1-V, Copy #7
CNO, Op-16-PT, Copy #8,#9
TAIC, NAS Anacostia (2), Copy #10,#11
(1 retain, for TAIC, 1 for MIS-G2).
OCSigO, Radar Branch, Copy #12
(Attn: Capt. Keely)

L. R. HIRD
Commander, U.S.N.
By Direction of Director
Naval Research Laboratory

REPORT OF JOINT ARMY-NAVY RADAR TESTS ON JAPANESE PAPER BALLOONS

1. Foreword:

The responsibility for these tests was divided between the Naval Airship Training and Experimental Command and the Camp Evans Signal Laboratory.

2. Authority:

a. CESL.

(1) Letter file SPSRB, from OCSigO, dated 1 February 1945, subject: "Japanese Balloons", to HQ, SCGSA.

(2) Letter file SPSRD, from OCSigO, dated 6 February 1945, subject: "Detection of Paper Balloons", to HQ, SCGSA.

b. Navy.

Confidential despatch from Bureau of Aeronautics to Chief, Naval Airship Training and Experimental Command, 022155, dated 3 February 1945.

3. Purpose:

To determine the reflectivity of captured Japanese paper balloons, exclusive of metal parts, for radar purposes.

4. Summary:

a. The results of the tests on the paper bag disclose the following maximum ranges in tracking the balloon:

Radio Set	Frequency	Range
SCR-545 (search)	200 Mc	7,700 yards
SCR-545 (track)	3000 Mc	24,000 yards
SCR-584	3000 Mc	33,000 yards
SCR-582	3000 Mc	5½ nautical miles*
AN/APS-2	3000 Mc	5½ nautical miles*
SCR-271	106 Mc	Did not make a positive identification at practical detection ranges.
AN/TPS-1	1100 Mc	
AN/TPS-3	600 Mc	
SCR-296	700 Mc	
AN/APS-15	X-Band	Target passed above elevation limit of the equipment.

* Target passed out of the lobe when balloon dropped to ground; does not represent maximum ranges.

b. The most satisfactory radar frequency for detection of the Japanese paper balloon (bag alone) is S-Band; no equipment in the lower frequencies indicated satisfactory detection ranges.

5. Conclusions:

a. The results of the free balloon test (exclusive of metal parts), on 28 February 1945, indicate that S-Band equipment will give the greatest range of detection. Results indicate that a weak reflection is obtained from the balloon on frequencies lower than the S-Band. On the X-Band, the limit of transmitted power will limit the range of detection.

b. The maximum expected range of the balloon on the S-Band is about 40% of the maximum range on a medium bomber.

c. An S-Band search set such as the AN/CPS-1 should give greater ranges of detection. With an increase of elevation of the lobe, coverage can be increased to the maximum altitude at which the balloons may be expected.

d. None of the present radar equipments will give entirely satisfactory area coverage, due to the weakness of the signal involved. The spacing of equipments required to cover a coastline would prohibit the use of the more complex radar sets except for coverage in a local area.

6. Recommendations:

a. It is recommended that tests be conducted using an AN/CPS-1 to determine the maximum range of detection of a Japanese balloon complete with metallic parts.

b. If further tests are conducted, it is suggested that a method of target identification be provided if possible, or that the balloon be released in the vicinity of the radar sets, thus allowing identification to be achieved by continuous plotting.

c. If it has not been done previously, it is suggested that a study of meteorological conditions in the Pacific Area be made to determine whether the balloons may be expected to follow a more or less predetermined path. By this means the strategic location of a few equipments might permit detection of a majority of the balloons.

7. Procedure:

a. Location of Tests. The tests on the paper balloon were conducted at Lakehurst Naval Air Station with various equipments located at or near that station as shown on the map attached as Enclosure No. 4.

b. Radar Equipment Utilized:

SCR-582 Mark III	SCR-545
AN/APS-2	SCR-296
AN/APS-15 on an airship	AN/TPS-1
	AN/TPS-3
two SCR-584's	two SCR-271's

c. Balloon. For test procedure and details regarding the balloon, see Enclosure No. 5.

d. Communications. The success or failure of tests of this type depends on communications, i.e., keeping in contact with the target and supplying bearings so the target may be located and identified. The radar stations and escorting aircraft were in contact with each other by means of radio and telephone. The balloon was accompanied on the first free flight by an airship from Lakehurst, and by a plane on the second free flight. The purpose of the aircraft was (1) to give a comparison echo with the balloon, (2) to indicate that the radar sets were functioning properly, (3) to give an approximate location of the balloon for detection purposes, and (4) the aircraft were also available to shoot the balloon down should it appear likely to land in a populated area.

8. Discussion:

a. A short summary of each of the balloon runs at Lakehurst and the data sheets of these runs, recorded by Radio Set SCR-584 and Radio Set SCR-545,

are attached as Enclosures No. 1, 2, and 3. Examination of the data discloses that the signal strength of the balloon (devoid of metal parts) is strongest in the S-Band frequency spectrums. The results were partially due to the fact that these equipments were located at Lakehurst Naval Air Station, and were able to get on target, and to follow the balloon to maximum range.

b. The lower frequency equipments were located at a remote distance from Lakehurst and were given the approximate position of the balloon by use of radio and telephone communications. They were unable to detect the target at any time, although all equipments detected aircraft and unidentified targets at equal and greater ranges.

c. It is believed that one of the main difficulties of detection for most radar sets of fixed elevation (SCR-296, SCR-582, AN/TPS-1, AN/TPS-3, and SCR-271) is the high altitude of the balloon path. Inspection of the coverage diagrams of these equipments shows that for the size of signal involved, the balloon will not be detected at a great enough distance nor at a high enough altitude to furnish information of any value.

d. Radio Set SCR-545-A tracked the balloon to 24,000 yar on the S-Band system, and Radio Set SCR-584 tracked it to 33,000 yards. These ranges are approximately 40% of the maximum ranges obtained by the respective sets on a medium bomber. The search system of the SCR-545-A (200 megacycles) had a weak signal to 7700 yards. This is approximately 10% of the range on a medium bomber. No information on ,ignal strength is available on the intermediate frequencies, but it is evident that there was no strong signal received.

e. No positive results were noted on the airborne X-Band equipment. This is due to the fact that the equipment could not be positioned properly to detect the balloon on its rapid rise. It is believed that the X-Band equipment could be successfully used to detect the balloons to ranges at least 40% of that to which a medium bomber can be tracked.

f. It is apparent from the ranges of Radio Sets SCR-584 and SCR-545 that for practical search a higher power set in the S-Band frequency is required. The S-Band set with enough power appears to be the AN/CPS-1 with approximately 800 kw peak power. Examination of the AN/CPS-1 polar diagram (see Enclosure No. 6) discloses detection range on a B-26 of 152 miles. Calculation on the basis of a 40% signal indicates a detection range of 60 - 75 miles. The height of the lobe is lower than the estimated 20,000 feet altitude at which the balloons are supposed to travel. To obtain maximum use of Radio Set AN/CPS-1 in the detection of these balloons, it is evident that the AN/CPS-1 beam should be tilted to 50, as indicated in Enclosure No. 6, to obtain coverage up to 35,000 feet altitude.

g. If altitude determination is necessary, the use of an equipment such as Radio Set AN/CPS-6 will be required. This set, like the AN/CPS-1, may also require an increase in the elevation angle of the antenna. However, it is doubtful whether the signal obtained will be sufficiently strong to permit high altitude determinations at a great enough range to permit interception.

CAPTIVE BALLOON - 20 February 1945

Radio Set	Frequency	Location & Distance from Captive Balloon	Remarks
AN/TPS-1	1080 Mc	Island Beach, N.J. Approx. range 19 miles.	Did not make a positive identification of the balloon.
SCR-296	700 Mc	CESL; 30,000 yards range.	Ground targets, probably hangers at Lakehurst, and several moving targets, probably airships, were detected, but no positive detection was made of the balloon.
SCR-584-B, #182	S-Band	CESL; 30,000 yards range.	Did not detect the balloon.
SCR-545-A, #85	200 Mc and	Lakehurst; 3100 yards range.	Troubled with fixed echoes could not identify balloon.
	S-Band		Troubled with fixed echoes; had saturated signal on balloon.
SCR-584-B #20	S-Band	Lakehurst; 3100 yards range.	Troubled by fixed echoes; received a saturated signal on the balloon.
SCR-582 Mark III	S-Band	Lakehurst; 1000 yards range.	Target could not be located, due to strong fixed echoes.
AN/APS-15	X-Band	Airship near Lakehurst.	Results not satisfactory, due to heavy ground echoes.
AN/APS-2	S-Band	Lakehurst; 1000 yards range.	Target could not be located, due to heavy fixed echoes.

Enclosure-1

REPORT OF JOINT ARMY-NAVY RADAR TESTS ON JAPANESE PAPER BALLOONS

FREE BALLOON - 20 February 1945

Radio Set	Frequency	Location	Remarks
AN/TPS-1	1080 Mc	Island Beach, N. J.	Picked up moving targets near Lakehurst believed to be airships and not balloon.
SCR-296	700 Mc	CESL	Detected several moving targets. Positions did not agree with position of balloon.
SCR-584-B, #182	S-Band	CESL	Picked up balloon at 29,000 yards and followed it to 22,000 yards, when balloon fell. S/N ratio 1.5/1 to 2/1.
SCR-545-A, #85	200 Mc and S-Band	Lakehurst	No signal. Picked up balloon at 7500 yards and tracked it to 11,250 yards, when it fell to the ground. S/N about 8/1.
SCR-584-B, #20	S-Band	Lakehurst	Tracked balloon for 14 minutes until it fell at 11,250 yards. Signal strong; tracked on automatic.
SCR-582 Mark III	S-Band	Lakehurst	Tracked balloon until it went down at approximately 5-1/2 nautical miles. Signal very good on PPI scope.
AN/APS-15	S-Band	Airship near Lakehurst	Results not satisfactory, due to ground echoes.
AN/APS-2	S-Band	Lakehurst	Tracked balloon until it went down. Signal strength very good on PPI scope.

Enclosure-2

Radio Set SCR-584-B, Serial No. 20, Free Balloon Test
20 February 1945 - Lakehurst Naval Air Station
Balloon Releaed at Approximately 1415 Hours

Time	El°	Az°	Slant Range (Yd)	Horizontal Range (Yd)	Alt (Ft)
1422	16.87	77.3	5500	5260	4780
1423	15.47	74.0	6500	6265	5200
1424	12.65	73.1	7000	6830	4670
1425	11.25	71.7	7500	7350	4380
1426	9.83	71.7	8500	8370	4350
1427	9.28	71.7	9000	8880	4350
1428	8.43	70.3	9500	9400	4180
1429	7.03	68.9	9700	9625	3560
1430	5.62	67.5	10,000	9950	2940
1431	4.22	66.1	10,250	10,220	2265
1432	2.81	66.1	10,500	10,490	1540
1433	2.08	64.7	11,000	10,992	1190
1434	2.08	64.7	11,100	11,092	1205
1435	1.40	64.7	11,150	11,146	816
1436	1.40	64.7	11,200	11,246	820

Note: S/N ratios could not be read accurately on Radio Set SCR-584.

Enclosure-2 (Contd)

Radio Set SCR-545-A, Serial No. 85, Free Balloon Test
20 February 1945 - Lakehurst Naval Air Station
Balloon Released at Approximately 1415 hours

Time	El°	Az°	Slant Range (Yd)	Horizontal Range (Yd)	Alt (Ft)	S/N
1424	15.83	72.5	7600	7310	6220	10/1
1425	9.11	72.5	8450	8340	4015	10/1
1426	8.16	72.5	9050	8950	3850	10/1
1427	7.09	70.9	9400	9325	3480	10/1
1428	6.36	69.7	9700	9640	3220	10/1
1429	5.06	68.1	10,050	10,020	2655	10/1
1430	3.66	66.8	10,300	10,280	1970	8/1
1431	2.42	66.0	10,600	10,590	1340	8/1
1432	1.97	65.4	10,900	10,890	1122	8/1
1433	0.85	65.1	11,250	11,250	501	8/1

Enclosure-2 (Contd)

REPORT OF JOINT ARMY-NAVY RADAR TESTS ON JAPANESE PAPER BALLOON

FREE BALLOON - 28 February 1945

Radio Set	Frequency	Location	Remarks
SCR-271	100 Mc	Oakhurst, N.J.	Detected moving targets. None identified as balloon.
SCR-271-DA	100 Mc	CESL	Did not detect balloon.
AN/TPS-3	600 Mc	CESL	Detected moving targets. Could not identify any as balloon.
SCR-296	700 Mc	CESL	Detected moving targets. Positions do not agree with position of balloon.
AN/TPS-1	1080 Mc	Island Beach, N. J.	Detected moving targets. Could not identify balloon.
SCR-584, #182	S-Band	CESL	Tracked target at high altitude, believed to be balloon. Positions do not agree with known position of balloon.
SCR-545-A, #85	200 Mc and	Lakehurst	Tracked target to 7700 yards with 1/1 signal.
	S-Band		See data. Tracked target to 24,000 yards.
SCR-584-B, #20	S-Band	Lakehurst	See data. Tracked target to 33,000 yards.
SCR-582	S-Band	Lakehurst	Tracked target to 2-1/2 nautical miles; then target passed above lobe.
AN/APS-15	X-Band	Airship near Lakehurst	Balloon rose above the airship before detection.
AN/APS-2	S-Band	Lakehurst	Reached excessive altitude before set could be brought to proper azimuth.

Enclosure-3

Radio Set SCR-584-B, Serial No. 20, Free Balloon Test
28 February 1945 - Lakehurst Naval Air Station
Balloon Released at 1100 Hours

Time	El°	Az°	Slant Range (Yd)	Horizontal Range (Yd)	Alt (Ft)	
1109	30.94	84.4	4600	3940	7100	
1110	30.94	81.5	5100	4420	7870	
1110½	29.53	78.7	6000	5226	8850	
1111	29.53	77.4	6300	5480	9300	
1111½	29.53	75.9	6600	5740	9740	
1112	29.53	74.5	6900	6010	10,180	
1112½	29.53	71.7	7300	6350	10,780	
1113	29.25	71.7	7900	6900	11,560	Note 1
1113½	28.97	70.3	8300	7275	12,030	
1114	28.12	70.3	8900	7850	12,580	
1114½	28.12	70.3	9300	8200	13,130	
1115	27.0	70.3	9700	8640	13,230	
1115½	27.0	70.3	10,400	9270	14,180	
1116	26.44	71.7	11,200	10,020	14,930	Note 2
1117	26.44	73.1	13,000	11,650	17,350	
1117½	25.31	75.4	14,200	12,830	18,200	
1118	24.19	77.4	15,000	13,700	18,350	Note 3
1118½	25.31	77.4	15,900	14,380	20,400	
1119	24.75	78.7	16,500	14,990	20,750	Note 4
1122	23.91	81.5	19,000	17,350	23,060	Note 5
1122½	23.91	83.0	20,000	18,280	24,300	
1123	23.62	83.0	22,000	20,160	26,400	
1123½	22.50	82.3	23,000	21,250	26,400	
1124	21.94	81.5	24,000	22,270	26,780	
1125	21.09	78.7	26,000	24,260	28,080	
1125½	20.25	77.4	27,000	25,390	28,050	
1126	20.25	77.4	29,000	27,200	30,100	
1126½	19.69	77.4	30,000	28,240	30,330	

Enclosure-3(Contd)

Time	El°	Az°	Slant Range (Yd)	Horizontal Range (Yd)	Alt (Ft)	
1127	19.69	77.4	31,000	29,190	31,300	
1127½	19.13	75.9	32,000	30,240	31,500	Note 6
1128	16.88	75.9	33,000	31,570	28,800	Note 7

Some readings were missed because of operators having to give bearings over phone.

Note 1. - No plane as yet.

Note 2. - No plane.

Note 3. - Signal growing fainter.

Note 4. - Plane in sight about 6000 yards behind balloon. Unable to get comparison check, too far behind and not directly on target.

Note 5. - Signal strength dropping off.

Note 6. - Tracking manually.

Note 7. - Lost target going out of range. Elevation of last reading may be in error.

S/N ratios could not be read accurately on SCR-584.

Enclosure-3 (Contd)

Radio Set SCR-545-A, Serial No. 85 - Free Balloon Test
28 February 1945 - Lakehurst Naval Air Station
Balloon Released at 1100 Hours

Time	El°	Az°	Slant Range (Yd)	Horizontal Range (Yd)	Alt (Ft)	Track S/N	Search S/N	
1109	29.93	84.3	4900	4240	7330	10/1		
1110	28.97	87.1	5600	4895	8140	10/1		
1111	28.86	84.1	6200	5430	8980	10/1	2/1	
1112	28.86	74.8	6900	6040	9980	10/1	1/1	
1113	28.30	72.2	7700	6780	10,950	9/1	1/1	Note 1,
1114	27.39	71.4	8750	7770	12,080	9/1		
1115	26.66	71.3	9800	8760	13,180	9/1		
1116	25.65	73.1	10,800	9730	14,020	8/1		
1117	25.37	72.7	11,950	10,800	15,360	5/1		
1118	24.24	74.2	13,500	12,300	16,600	2/1		
1119	23.96	76.7	15,200	13,880	18,530	2/1		
1120	23.79	78.7	16,400	15,000	19,850	2/1		
1121	23.51	81.1	18,000	16,500	21,550	1/1		Note 2
1122	22.73	83.2	19,650	18,120	22,750	1/1		
1123	21.94	83.5	22,000	20,380	24,650	1/1		Note 3
1124	21.49	82.9	24,000	22,300	26,350	½/1		

Plane which was supposed to be circling balloon was seen only once. No comparative check could be made.

Note 1. - Target disappeared in search scope.

Note 2. - Signal jittery.

Note 3. - Signal very jittery.

Enclosure-3 (Contd)

TEST DATA MEMORANDUM
AIRSHIP EXPERIMENTAL DEPARTMENT
NAVAL AIR STATION, LAKEHURST, N. J.

C O N F I D E N T I A L

TDM No. 94
Date 7 Mar. 1945.

TEST: Radar Test of Inflated Paper Balloon - Condition, Repair, Inflation and Flight of Balloons.

AUTHORITY: (a) BuAer conf dispatch to CNATE 022155 February.
(b) CNATE T.O. No. 153.

OBJECT: To determine Radar detection range of an inflated paper balloon.

ENCLOSURES: 1. Lakehurst photographs L.H. Nos. 22269, 22274, and 22277 - First Paper Balloon Flown - Captive.

2. Lakehurst photographs L.H. Nos. 22345, 22344, 22346, 22348, and 22349 - Inflation and Free Flight of Second Balloon.

WITNESSES: Lt. (jg) R.W. Sims, USNR, Balloon Officer.

CONCLUSIONS/RECOMMENDATIONS

(a) The first paper balloon was wet, without protective varnish, and badly mildewed and torn when received. After being dried out, it became porous, hard and brittle, and some of the panel seams opened up during drying. This indicates that the paper and glue may lose their water-proof characteristics under certain prolonged conditions of temperature and moisture changes.

(b) The paper balloons, when in good condition, can easily be inflated under no wind conditions, such as in a hangar, when the lifting gas under 5 to 10 pounds pressure is added from a helium truck or valve through a fabric sleeve and a fabric inflation appendix, which is installed on the balloon. Also, these balloons can easily be "walked" when inflated, from a hangar to a cleared area for take-off with wind gusts under 10 knots (see Encl. 2).

(c) The balloons can also be inflated in the open in a similar manner at wind gusts under 8 knots, but inflation is extremely difficult when the gusts are above 8 knots.

(d) Weather conditions, such as surface and upper wind velocity; direction and the visibility should be accurately known before flying the balloon for radar tests. For future tests, it is recommended that an aerology balloon with corner reflector be tracked to determine the weather conditions.

(e) Good communications between radar stations, crew releasing the balloon, and aircraft following it, are essential for good radar results.

(f) In order to study radar signal strength, the balloon may be flown captive either with the catenary foot ropes or standard balloon net attached to a line. Using a balloon in good condition, with surface winds less than 10 knots, and the procedure shown in Encl. 1, altitudes of 2000 feet or greater can be obtained.

(g) It is believed that the inflation of the balloon can be accomplished in a very small area, such as the hold of a ship. Also, from the construction of the balloon, it appears likely that the gas is added through the valve hole, the valve secured, and the balloon released without much movement.

DETAILS OF TEST

APPARATUS:

(a) First Test - Balloon Captive: First paper balloon, 17,000 cu. ft. volume; material to repair balloon (commer[illegible] pa[illegible] gl[illegible]); standard

Enclosure-5

TEST: Radar Test of Inflated Paper Balloon - Condition, Repair, Inflation and Flight of Balloons.

19,000 cu. ft. free balloon net; 500 ft. coil of nylon line, ½" dia.; 2200 ft. coil of 5/32" steel cable on a reel; a Macon winch; fabric inflation sleeve; fabric inflation appendix; and helium supply.

(b) Second Test - Balloon Free Flight: First paper balloon; balloon net; sand bags (20 lb.); and helium truck.

(c) Third Test - Balloon Free Flight: Second paper balloon, 17,000 cu. ft. volume; fabric inflation appendix; sand bags (20 lb.); and helium supply.

PROCEDURE: The first 17,000 cu ft. enemy paper balloon received at this station was wet, badly mildewed, torn, and contained numerous holes. The balloon was dried, and it was observed that some of the panel seams opened up during the drying period. After drying, all holes, tears and opened seams were repaired, using commercial kraft paper with casein glue as the adhesive. No attempt was made to restore the protective varnish where that had disappeared from the balloon, nor was any such protective coating applied over the rather extensive repaired areas. Finally, a 6" diameter fabric inflation appendix was installed for inflation purposes. (Photo. 22345, Encl. 2).

The balloon was inflated with helium on Feb. 14, 1945, under a standard 19,000 cu. ft. free balloon net. The balloon collapsed about 3 hours after inflation due to the porosity of the paper.

For the first test, it was considered desirable to study the radar signal strength from the paper balloon, which, it was thought, could be accomplished by flying the balloon as a captive at approximately 2,000 feet altitude. On 20 Feb. the balloon, under the net, was inflated with approximately 10,000 cu. ft. of helium. A 500 ft. coil of ½" diameter nylon line was placed on a Macon winch which was secured to an open platform truck. An additional 2200 ft. coil of 5/32" steel cable on a separate reel was also placed on the truck. The balloon and truck were moved to a clear area, the nylon line attached to the balloon which was then released, and after about 400 ft. of line had been reeled out, the tethering cable was attached as shown by Photo #22274, Encl. 1. The balloon ascended to approximately 600-1000 ft. and after a period of about an hour, descended due to loss of helium, caused by the porosity of the paper. The wind was west, 15 knots.

From the results obtained, and due to the wind being in the direction toward Camp Evans, it was decided in the second test to release the balloon on a free flight. The balloon, which by this time was in very bad condition, due to large holes that could not be repaired, was inflated (still under net) to 9,000 cu. ft. on the field, using helium from a truck. An effort was made to remove the net; however, the wind was gusty (to 20 knots), and in order to prevent further damage to the balloon, it was released (without valve or metal attachments) with about 8 sand bags still attached. The balloon rose rapidly to an altitude of 4500 feet (SW wind, 25 to 30 knots), as determined by an L-ship which was assigned to track the balloon and shoot it down if it got out of range (in the direction of populated areas) of a truck which was also assigned to follow it. After being in the air about 30 minutes, the balloon lost enough lift to settle into the trees at a distance of about 5-1/2 miles from the take-off point. The Balloon, when recovered, was in such a damaged condition as to preclude the possibility of making further tests with it and because of the classification, it has been stored awaiting further disposition.

On 28 Feb., a second flight (third test) was made, using another paper balloon which was in much better condition than the first balloon. That is, the paper was not porous, held helium well, and the balloon did not appear to have been wet. The balloon was inflated to 8,000 cu. ft. with the valve set at a reduced opening pressure, and the inflation line left open. For this flight the valve

TEST: Radar Test of Inflated Paper Balloon - Condition, Repair, Inflation and Flight of Balloons.

---

was left attached, because it was believed that without it, the helium would escape too rapidly and thus shorten the flight. The balloon was inflated using the outside catenary, which is part of the balloon, and tied off at the foot ropes using a 20 lb. sand bag to maintain tension on the foot ropes (Encl. 2). Weather conditions were, 15 knots of surface wind from the west, increasing to 70-80 knots at between 15,000 and 20,000 feet. After release, the balloon ascended slowly until it reached an altitude of approximately 1,000 ft. At the altitude, the wind increased and the flight path of the balloon was due east of the station, and within the line of sight of the radar stations.

An SNJ airplane, which was assigned to follow and circle the balloon (comparative radar targets), and to shoot it down in the event it headed toward a populated area, lost sight of it due to poor visibility when the balloon was about 10 miles at sea, at an altitude in excess of the plane's ceiling. The balloon was headed due east at approximately 70 knots air speed, and it presumably went down at sea some distance from shore.

RESULTS: The flights of the balloons are believed satisfactory, because a good target for the radar was provided. The radar results and data are contained in report of Joint Army-Navy Radar Tests on Japanese Paper Balloon of 7 March.

DISCUSSION: The first two flights of the balloon were not as good as desired, primarily because of the condition of the balloon. The third flight is believed as good as can be expected. It is possible that more ballast could have been added, causing the balloon to reach static equilibrium sooner, and thus fly at a lower altitude. However, this would probably have shortened the balloon's flight The valve could also have been left off, but due to the oscillating motion of the balloon in flight, it is believed that the helium would have leaked out, causing the balloon to descend after a short flight.

Helium was used for the inflation gas instead of hydrogen, because of: the difficulties involved in inflation, no enclosed space available where hydrogen could be handled safely, hazards to personnel, and it was not considered wise to release a pilotless balloon of this capacity, filled with hydrogen, free on an unpredictable course. All experience gained at this station using the radar to detect hydrogen and helium filled aerology or small paper balloons indicate that there is no difference in the signals obtained.

s/ E. W. Harrison
E. W. HARRISON, Lieut., USNR,
Test Engineer.

s/ B. F. Jenkins
B. F. JENKINS, Capt., USN(Ret.),
Director, Experimental & Flight Test Dept.

Enclosure-5 (Contd)

M E M O R A N D U M

22 February 1945

From: LTA Design.
To: Op-16-V-T.

Subj: Japanese Paper Balloons - Possible Size of.

1. The Japanese paper balloons so far reported are about 32 feet in diameter, and 17,200 cubic foot volume. One limitation upon the possible size of these balloons is the strength of the paper to resist the gas pressure at the top of the balloons. This limit does not appear to be approached by the balloons now coming over. The following table shows the sizes and load capacities of the current balloons designated A, and two hypothetical balloons, B and C. Balloon B is the largest size which it is calculated could be made of the same paper as balloon A, and C is the largest size using a paper of double the strength and unit weight of that in the A and B balloons.

Designation		A	B	C
Diameter	ft.	32.0	62.6	111.8
Volume	cu.ft.	17,200	128,400	731,500
Gross lift at 30,000 ft.	lbs.	447	3340	19,020
Gross lift at 40,000 ft.	lbs.	292	2180	12,400
Weight of balloon with valve and rigging	lbs.	152	705	4325
Useful load at 30,000 ft.	lbs.	295	2635	14,695
Useful load at 40,000 ft.	lbs.	140	1475	8,075

NOTE: Useful load includes equipment, bombs, ballast, and ballast dropping device.

2. Probably balloon B is about the largest practicable size from other considerations than strength. Inflation of a larger balloon would present considerable difficulties. According to Lieutenant Tanner of NRL it is probably feasible to make paper twice as strong and of the same strength/weight ratio as in the A and B balloons, but it would be about 8 times as stiff, and would be difficult to handle or fold without cracking.

3. According to the Bureau of Standards (letr. V-3/Ic 136c of 1/17/45) the tensile strength of the paper is greatly affected by the relative humidity and has the following values:

Relative Humidity	Tensile Strength lb/linear in.
30%	66
65%	46
100%	21
Weight	4.8 oz./sq.yd.

It is believed reasonable to design for a continuous load of 14 lb/in (= 168 lb/ft) giving a margin of 0.5 at 100 % humidity and 2.3 at 65% humidity. At high altitude the relative humidity should rarely exceed 65%.

4. The automatic gas valves of the present balloons are set to open at a pressure of 1.67" of water. It is assumed that the maximum super-pressure would be 1.75" of water, or 9.10 lb/sq.ft. The gas pressure at the top of the balloon is given by:

$$p = p_o + 2Rk$$

where p = gas pressure at top.
p_o = super-pressure = 9.10 lb/ft^2
R = radius of the balloon
k = unit lift of the gas

The unit lift of 97.5% pure hydrogen is 0.0695 lb/ft^3 in standard atmosphere at sea level. From the loads known to be carried by the balloons, it is calculated that the initial inflation is 37.4%, which gives a pressure height of 30,000 feet. At that altitude, k = 0.026 lb/ft^3. This value is assumed in the calculations of the sizes of the B and C balloons.

5. The tension in the fabric at the top of the balloon due to the gas pressure is given by:

$$T = Rp/2$$
$$= (R/2)(p_o + 2Rk)$$

or

$$R^2k + Rp_o/2 - T = 0$$

It is assumed that T = 168 lb/ft for balloon B, and T = 336 lb/ft for balloon C. From expression $R^2k + Rp_o/2 - T = 0$, the limiting values of R are 31.3 feet and 55.9 feet, respectively.

6. It is possible that too great an allowable strength in the paper has been assumed in the foregoing calculations. There is some reason for believing that the strength may be rather erratic, and the capacity for sustained load so much less than the tensile strength developed in a quick breaking test that the margins allowed are not sufficient. Further examination and tests of the paper might throw more light on the matter and lead to a revision of the estimates of the limiting sizes of the balloons. The revision would more probably be downward rather than upward.

C. P. BURGESS

Aer-E-191-CPB
F1(1)

May 1945

Design Memorandum No. 371.

Small, Long Range Spherical Balloons.

by

C. P. Burgess.

- -

Summary.

The minimum size of a spherical balloon to remain at high altitudes for about 5 days with a useful load of one pound is investigated. It is found that the size increases very rapidly with the weight of the fabric. With fabric weighing 1 oz./yd.^{2}, the balloon need be only 7.9 ft. in diameter, but with fabric at 5 oz./yd.^{2} the required diameter is 26.8 ft.

Paper or impregnated cloth fabrics are probably impracticable for less weight than 4.0 oz./yd.^{2}. which calls for a balloon 21.7 ft. in diameter.

Cellophane is ideal for a 1.0 oz./yd.^{2} fabric in all respects except that it becomes as brittle as glass at stratosphere temperatures. Possibly a similar material without this fatal objection can be developed.

Calculation of Minimum Size.

Let V = volume of balloon, cu. ft.

" S = surface area, sq. ft.

" D = diameter, ft.

" W = gross weight, lbs.

" W_b = weight of ballast and ballast dropping device, lbs.

" W_a = weight of fabric and rigging, including valve, lbs.

" W_u = useful load, lbs.

" $k = W_a/S$

" $W = W_a + W_b + W_u$ - (1)

" $V = (\pi/6)D^3 \qquad V^{2/3} = 0.65D^2$

" $S = \pi D^2 = 4.83V^{2/3}$

" $W_a = 4.83kV^{2/3}$ - (2)

" $W_u = 1.0$ lb. - (3)

It is assumed on the basis of the analysis in Design Memo No. 368 that the weight of ballast required is 50% of the initial gross lift, and the ballast dropping device weighs 5% of the gross lift, whence:

$W_b = 0.55W$ - (4)

Substituting (2), (3), and (4) in (1) and re-arranging:

$$W = 4.83kV^{2/3} + 0.55W + 1.0$$

$$0.45W = 4.83kV^{2/3} + 1.0 \text{ - (5)}$$

The balloon is required to have an initial ceiling of about 30,000 ft., corresponding to a sea level inflation of 37%. With gas lifting 0.070 lb./ft.^{3} at sea level,

$$W = 0.070 \times 0.37V = 0.026V \text{ - (6)}$$

From (5) and (6),

$$0.0117V = 4.83kV^{2/3} + 1.0 \text{ - (7)}$$

In order to allow for the weight of the seams and rigging, it is assumed that k is 50% greater than the weight of the fabric per unit area. Since k is expressed in lb./ft.^{2}, its magnitude is 1.5/144 = 0.01042 times the weight of the fabric in ounces/sq. yd.

The characteristics of balloons with fabric weighing from 1.0 to 5.0 oz/yd.^{2} have been calculated from expression (7) and are shown in the following table:

Weight of fabric						
	oz./yd.^{2}	1.0	2.0	3.0	4.0	5.0
k,	lb./ft.^{2}	.01042	.02084	.03126	.04168	.05210
V	ft.^{3}	262	858	2380	5350	10100
D	ft.	7.9	11.8	16.6	21.7	26.8
S	ft.^{2}	196	437	866	1480	2260
W_a	lb.	2.05	9.0	26.9	61.5	117.0
W_b	lb.	3.75	12.3	34.0	76.5	144.5
W_u	lb.	1.00	1.0	1.0	1.0	1.0
W	lb.	6.80	22.3	61.9	139.0	262.5
W_u/W	%	14.7	4.5	1.62	0.72	0.38

It is apparent that the volume is very sensitive to the weight of the fabric. If the useful load were zero, the volume would vary as the cube of the weight of the fabric per unit area.

On the other hand, with heavy fabric, the useful load can be greatly increased without much increase in the volume. For example, with 5.0 ounce fabric, and increase of useful load from 1.0 lb. to 33.0 lb. requires a balloon of 17,300 cu. ft. volume with an initial gross weight of 450 lb. The ratio of useful load to gross weight is increased from 0.38% to 7.3%. Such a balloon approximates to the paper balloons discussed in Design Memo No. 368.

It is considered improbable that a satisfactory paper fabric can be made lighter than about 4.0 oz./yd.^{2}. A balloon constructed of such heavy material would be a very uneconomical carrier for a one pound useful load.

A material similar to cellophane would be ideal for very small balloons provided embrittlement at stratosphere temperatures could be avoided, and a satisfactory seaming technique developed. Cellophane 8.8×10^{-4} inch

in thickness has a minimum tensile strength of about 25 lb./in. at 75° F. and 35% relative humidity, and weighs only 1.02 oz./yd.^{2}. The rate of diffusion of hydrogen is said to be less than o.1 liter/m^2/day, or 3.28×10^{-4} ft./day. The corresponding loss of lift for the smallest balloon in the above table is only

$$3.28 \times 10^{-4} \times 192 \times 0.026 = 1.64 \times 10^{-3} \text{ lb./day.}$$

This is negligible, and there will probably be fewer pin hole imperfections in cellophane than in a paper or impregnated cloth fabric.

It is probable that the transparency of cellophane would cause less superheat than with an opaque fabric; and it might also be a less effective radar target.

Cellophane has very low tear resistance, and great care must be taken in handling a balloon made of it, but there should be but little hazard from this source after take-off.

In view of the very low rate of gas diffusion and possibly low degree of superheat, it might be possible for a cellophane balloon to make a flight of five days with less than 50% of ballast. If the ballast on the 7.8 ft. diameter balloon could be reduced one-half, the useful load could be increased from 1.0 lb. to 2.875 lb., or 42% of the gross lift. On the other hand, a few pin holes or imperfections in the seams of such a small balloon might greatly increase the daily loss of lift.

In spite of its nearly ideal characteristics for small balloons, cellophane is unsuitable for high altitude operation because it becomes nearly as brittle as glass at stratosphere temperatures; but there is the possibility that a similar material without this characteristic may be developed. There is also the alternative possibility of an elastic material having the light weight and low permeability of cellophane. A balloon constructed of such a material might be contained in a net of strong thread to secure the constant volume feature necessary for stability. Rubber and neoprene are not suitable materials because their permeabilities and rates of deterioration in sunlight are far too high for a five day flight.

Operation

It is believed that the best ballast for an unmanned free balloon is a non-freezing liquid in a container with an automatic device designed to release a small quantity of ballast when the balloon becomes less than completely full of gas, regardless of altitude after the initial ascent to pressure height. With a simple gas pressure relief valve set to hold a pressure of about 2" of water, the balloon would be stable between the height of fullness and pressure height as discussed in Design Memo No. 368. If the ballasting device releases ballast as soon as the balloon is less than fully inflated, the flight path will not have the 3,000 ft. dips below pressure height which occur with the paper balloons in which the release of ballast is controlled by an aneroid which does not drop an increment of ballast until the balloon has descended 3,000 ft. below the last peak of altitude.

Aer-E-191-CPB
F1(1)

CONFIDENTIAL

April, 1945

Design Memorandum No. 368.

The Endurance of a Free Balloon with Automatic Pressure and Ballast Controls.

by

C. P. Burgess

C. P. Burgess

****

Summary.

It is shown that an unmanned free balloon with a gas valve set to hold 1.75" of water pressure and an automatic ballast dropping device can stay in the air from 4.2 to 6.5 days in favorable conditions. The secret of this exceptional endurance lies in the use of a gas valve which insures a zone of stability between the altitude at which the balloon is just full, and the altitude at which the valve opens.

The calculations are necessarily based upon assumptions which may need revision in the light of more complete information on the rate of gas leakage and the degree of superheat during the day.

The Balloons

Two sizes of spherical balloons are assumed. The smaller one is 31.8 ft. in diameter, and 16,800 cu. ft. in volume. The larger one is 33.3 ft. in diameter, and 19,300 cu. ft. in volume. Both balloons weigh 216.0 lb. empty, and carry 35 increments of ballast, each weighing 5.5 lb., and one 33 lb. center load, making an initial gross weight of 441.5 lb. After dropping 192.5 lb. of ballast the gross weight is 249 lb.

It is assumed that the balloons are inflated with dry hydrogen, 97.5% pure, having a unit lift of 0.0695 lb./ft.^{3} at sea level in the standard atmosphere. The required initial inflations for equilibrium are:

Small balloon:
441.5/(16,800x.0695) = 37.8%

Large balloon:
441.5/(19,300x.0695) = 32.9%

The corresponding altitudes at which the balloons will be just full in the standard atmosphere are 29,700 ft. and 33,400 ft., respectively, for the small and large balloons.

After dropping all ballast the inflations at sea level are:

Small balloon:
249/(16,800x.0695) = 21.3%

Large balloon:
249/(19,300x.0695) = 18.6%

The corresponding altitudes of fullness are 42,900 ft. and 45,750 ft., respectively, for the small and large balloons.

The balloons are fitted with automatic gas pressure relief valves, set to open at a pressure of 1.75" of water (=9.1 lb./sq.ft.).

The ballast dropping device is designed to drop one 5.5 lb. increment of ballast whenever the balloon falls about 3,000 ft. below the last peak in its vertical oscillations.

Conditions of Flight.

Approximately standard atmospheric conditions with no appreciable vertical currents are assumed to prevail throughout the flight. Since the vertical motions are rather slow, except in the initial ascent, the stabilizing effect of possible adiabatic changes in the gas temperature are neglected. The point is not important because it is shown that the balloon is stable between the height of fullness and pressure height.

It is assumed that there is no superheat during the night. The two conditions of 30° F. and 45° F. superheat during the day are investigated. These superheats may be on the low side. The report on the flight of the National Geographic Society's stratosphere balloon recorded 108° F. superheat at 73,000 ft. altitude, but the pilot suggested that the observed gas temperature may have been above the true mean temperature because of the proximity of the gas thermometer to the surface of the envelope. It is also possible that the paper fabric of the balloons here considered would absorb less heat than the rubberized cotton cloth of the stratosphere balloon. On the other hand, the smaller size of the paper balloons would probably tend to increase the superheat.

Duration of Flight.

It will be shown that the pressure of 1.75" H_2O at which the gas pressure relief valve opens provides sufficient stability to prevent the balloon from overshooting pressure height and losing gas by valving during the normal vertical oscillations caused by dropping the increments of ballast. Gas will be valved only as a result of the daily superheat. 30° F. superheat expands the valume of the gas 7.6% at constant pressure. It can be assumed that 1% of the expansion will be taken care of by increased pressure and leakage, leaving 6.6% of the gross lift to be valved per day. The amounts to 29 lb./day at the beginning of the flight, and 16.5 lb./day at the end, or an average of 22.7 lb./day. With 45° F. superheat the mean daily loss by valving is 36 lb./day.

The loss of lift by leakage of gas is assumed to be 12 lb./day as a minimum and 24 lb./day as a maximum. The possible duration of the flight in days is obtained by dividing the 192.5 lbs. of ballast by the daily loss of lift, and adding one day for the initial ascent and final descent. From these data, the following combinations are obtained:

Superheat	°F	30		45	
Loss of lift by valving, lb./day		22.7	22.7	36	36
Loss of lift by leakage lb./day		12.0	24.0	12	24
Total loss of lift, lb./day		34.7	46.7	48	60
Endurance	days	6.5	5.1	5.0	4.2

Dropping a possible 33 lb. load during the final descent would cause the balloon to shoot far up above its pressure height and lose so much gas that it would fall rapidly thereafter.

Symbols.

The following symbols are used in the theoretical analysis of the motion of the balloon, and the computation of the daily loss of gas:

V - maximum volume of the balloon, cu. ft.
m - virtual mass, lb.sec.^{2}/ft.
h - altitude above sea level, ft.

Δh = [illegible] altitude, or specifically the height between the altitude at [illegible] the balloon is just full, and pressure height.
t = time, seconds.
p = density of the ambient atmosphere, $lb.sec.^2/ft.^4$
gp = specific weight of the air, $lb./ft.^3$
p = relative gas pressure in the balloon, $lb./ft.^2$
v = dh/dt = vertical velocity, ft./sec.
a = d^2h/dt^2 = acceleration, $ft./sec.^2$
F = free lift, lb.
dF/dt = rate of change of free lift, lb./sec.
K = air resistance of the balloon divided by v^2.
C = rate of change of gross lift with altitude, lb./ft.

Since the balloon has a gas pressure relief valve which does not open until the relative pressure at the bottom of the balloon is 9.1 $lt./ft.^2$, it is important to distinguish between the height of fullness at which the balloon is fully inflated without super-pressure, and the pressure height at which the super-pressure is 9.1 $lb./ft.^2$ It will be shown that the stability of the balloon between these two altitudes is the key to its long endurance.

Neglecting vertical air currents and changes of superheat, the equation of motion of the full balloon is:

$$K(dh/dt)^2 + m\ (d^2h/dt^2) - F + C\Delta h = 0$$

This may also be written:

$$Kv^2 + ma - F + C\Delta h = 0 \quad \text{- - - - - - - - - - - - - - - - - -} \quad (1)$$

The first term represents the air resistance to vertical velocity, with K varying as p.

The second term is the virtual mass times the acceleration.

The third term is the difference between gross buoyancy and gross weight, counted positive when buoyancy is the greater.

The fourth term is the change of buoyancy with altitude multiplied by the change of altitude. Between the height of fullness and pressure height:

$$C = Vd(gp)/dh$$

d(gp)/dh is taken from the N.A.C.A. standard atmosphere tables.

The total range of altitude between fullness and pressure height is given by:

$$\Delta h = p/gp = 9.1/gp$$

The change of buoyancy within the range Δh is given by:

$$-\Delta F = C\Delta h$$

Values of Δh, C, ΔF and K at various altitudes are given in the following table. Where two values are given for the same variable, the first refers to the 16,800 cu. ft. balloon, and the second to the 19,300 cu. ft. one. It may be noted that C and ΔF vary as V, and K as $V^{2/3}$.

h	ft.	0	10,000	20,000	30,000	40,000	50,000
Δh	ft.	119	161	223	318	486	783
C	lb/ft.	.0376	.0298	.0234	.0177	.0150	.0093
		.0432	.0343	.0268	.0204	.0172	.0107
ΔF	lb.	4.47	4.80	5.22	5.63	7.28	7.29
		5.14	5.52	5.98	6.49	8.36	8.38
K	$\frac{\text{lb.sec}^2}{\text{ft.}^2}$	.364	.268	.194	.137	.089	.056
		.400	.295	.213	.150	.098	.061

Stretch of the fabric with increasing pressure will decrease C and increase Δh, but will not affect ΔF.

The virtual mass, M, is 1.5 times the actual mass of the balloon. Its initial value for both balloons is 1.5 x 441.5/32.2 = 20.6 lb. sec.^{2}/ft.

The terminal velocity is given by

$$v' = \sqrt{F/K}$$

When an upward force is suddenly applied by the dropping of ballast, the terminal velocity is never quite reached, but it is approached very closely within a short time and change of altitude. From (1) when C = 0,

$$Kv^2 + m\, dv/dt = F$$

$$dt/dv = m/(F-Kv^2)$$

$$\Delta h = \int v dt = \int v(dt/dv)\, dv$$

$$= m \int \frac{v dv}{F-Kv^2} = -\frac{m}{2K} \log_e (F/K-v^2) + A = 0 \text{ when } v = 0$$

$$A = (m/2K) \log_e F/K$$

$$\Delta h = (m/2K) \log_e \left\{(F/K)/(F/K-v^2)\right\} \text{ - - - - - - - - - - - - (2)}$$

Example: Let F = 4 lb.
" m = 20 lb.sec^2/ft.
" K = 0.20 lb.sec.^{2}/ft.^{2}

When $v = 0.9v' = \sqrt{0.81F/K}$

$$\frac{F/K}{F/K-v^2} = \frac{1}{1-0.81} = 5.26$$

$$\Delta h = 50 \log_e 5.26 = 83 \text{ ft.}$$

When a balloon falls below the altitude of fullness by gradual loss of lift from leakage of gas, the acceleration is negligible, and the loss of altitude is given by

$$-\Delta h = \int v\,dt = \int \sqrt{F/K}\,dt$$

$$= \sqrt{\frac{dF/dt}{K}} \int \sqrt{t}\,dt$$

$$= \frac{2}{3} \sqrt{\frac{dF/dt}{D}}\, t^{3/2} \quad \text{- - - - - - - - - - - - - - - - - - -(3)}$$

In this expression, dF/dt is the rate of loss of lift, and is assumed to be a constant independent of t.

The Flight

The probable course of a 19,300 cu. ft. balloon in terms of altitude versus time will now be investigated in detail. It is assumed that the daily superheat is 45° F., and the loss of lift by gas leakage is 24 lb./day, i.e., dF/dt = (1/3600) lb./sec.

The balloon takes off late in the afternoon, weighed off to be in equilibrium near pressure height after loss of superheat. The initial superheat will take it up rapidly at first, but with diminishing velocity as the gas is cooled by adiabatic expansion and the setting of the sun. The initial altitude of fullness is 33,400 ft., and pressure height is 375 ft. higher. It is assumed that the balloon comes to rest in equilibrium at 33,750 ft. altitude about 3 hours after the start of the flight. It then loses gas slowly by leakage, but it does not lose buoyancy or altitude until it ceases to be fully inflated. In other words, the altitude of fullness creeps up to the balloon as it loses its internal pressure, instead of the balloon descending to that level; but the time taken for this to occur can be calculated as if the balloon descended through the height Δh by loss of lift corresponding to the loss of gas.

$$t = \frac{C\,\Delta h}{dF/dt}$$

At 34,000 ft. altitude,

C = .0194 lb./ft. $\quad\Delta h$ = 350 ft.
K = 0.13 $\quad$ dF/dt = (1/3600) lb./sec.
t = .0194x350x3600 = 24,500 sec. = 6.8 hours.

When the balloon is at the altitude of fullness, further loss of gas will cause it to descend until the first increment of ballast is automatically dropped after a descent of 3,000 ft. To find the time of this descent we apply expression (3), as follows:

$$t^{3/2} = 1.5\Delta h \sqrt{\frac{K}{dF/dt}}$$

$$= 1.5 \times 3000 \times \sqrt{.130 \times 3600} = 97{,}500$$

$$t = 2100 \text{ sec.} = 35 \text{ min.}$$

The heaviness at this time is given by:

$$-\Delta F = t\,(dF/dt) = 2100/3600$$
$$= 0.58 \text{ lb.}$$

Dropping 5.5 lb. of ballast makes the balloon 4.92 lb. light. This will cause it to rise with a terminal velocity given by:

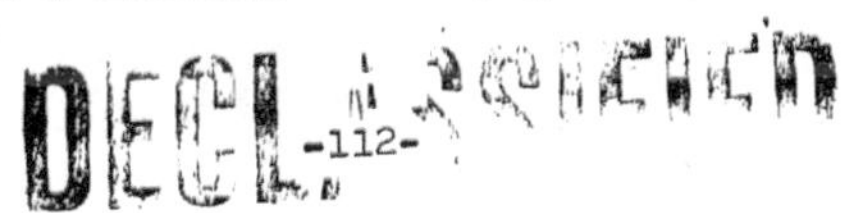

$$v' = \sqrt{F/K} = \sqrt{4.92/0.13} = 6.5 \text{ ft./sec.}$$

This velocity will return the balloon to the height of fullness in about 8 minutes.

The altitude of equilibrium is at 4.92/C = 4.92/.0194 = 254 ft. above the level of fullness, but owing to the kinetic energy resulting from the upward velocity, the balloon will overshoot the equilibrium position, and come substantially to rest after a few strongly damped oscillations. The maximum height above fullness can be calculated by equating the kinetic energy to the work done against gravity and the air resistance, as follows:

$$\text{Kinetic energy} = mv^2/2 = 20.3x(6.15)^2/2 = 385 \text{ ft. lb.}$$

The mean air resistance is $Kv^2/2 = 0.13x(615)^2/2 = 2.46$ lb., and the work done against it is $2.46\Delta h$, where Δh is the maximum height reached above the level of fullness.

The gravitational force is 0.0194h - 4.92, and the work done against gravity is given by

$$\int_0^{\Delta h} (.0194h - 4.92)\, dh = .0097(\Delta h)^2 = 4.92\Delta h$$

Equating the work to the kinetic energy gives:

$$0.0097(\Delta h)^2 - 2.46\,\Delta h - 385 = 0$$

Whence: $\Delta h = 363$ ft.

This is only about 12 ft. below pressure height, but the actual margin will be somewhat more because of the adiabatic cooling of the gas in the rapid rise. However, the calculation indicates that the 5.5 lb. increment of ballast is very close to the upper limit if the balloon is not to overshoot pressure height and lose gas by valving on the rise.

After the balloon levels off in equilibrium at 250 ft. above fullness it remains at a constant altitude while the height of fullness creeps up to it because of diminishing internal pressure from leakage of gas. The length of this period is given by:

$$t = C\Delta h/(dF/dt) = .0192x250x3600$$

$$= 17{,}280 \text{ sec.} = 288 \text{ min.}$$

Adding 43 minutes for the balloon to descend to the ballast dropping level and to return to equilibrium gives 331 minutes, or one minute longer than the 5.5 hours which must obviously be the length of the cycle between dropping the 5.5 lb. increments of ballast when the loss of lift by leakage is one lb. per hour and there is no change of superheat.

In each cycle the altitudes of fullness and equilibrium increase by the amount t(dF/dt)/C because of the loss of gas.

We shall now investigate the effect of superheat. It is not known how rapidly the superheating will occur, but it will probably take several hours. At the absolute temperature of 392.4° F. prevailing in the stratosphere above 35,300 ft. altitude, 45° F. superheat will expand the gas 11.5%. It can be assumed that about 1% will be handled by increased pressure in the balloon and by leakage of gas during superheating, and that 10.5% of the gas in the balloon at the beginning of the superheating will be removed by valving. The superheating causes no appreciable change in the lift or altitude of the balloon, and after the maximum temperature has been reached, the balloon resumes its normal oscillations with a 5.5 hour period. About 24 hours after the start of the flight the balloon begins to lose superheat, and during the cooling off period loses about 50 lb. of lift, including the loss by gas leakage. This requires the dropping of 9 increments of ballast in a time that probably does not exceed three hours. Between each release of ballast the balloon returns to the altitude of equilibrium, but soon begins to fall again as the cooling continues. During these oscillations, the altitude of fullness and pressure height rise about 2500 ft. because of the contraction of the gas.

After completely cooling off, the balloon resumes its normal vertical oscillations with a 5.5 hour period until the morning superheating begins, but since the balloon on the last rise after cooling will be only about 150 ft. above the altitude of fullness, it will again be at that level and begin its first 3000 ft. dip about 3 hours after cooling ceases.

The vertical motion of the balloon is plotted against time in the accompanying figure. One increment of ballast is dropped at each oscillation. After the thirty-fifth oscillation the balloon descends to the ground.

Design Memo. 368

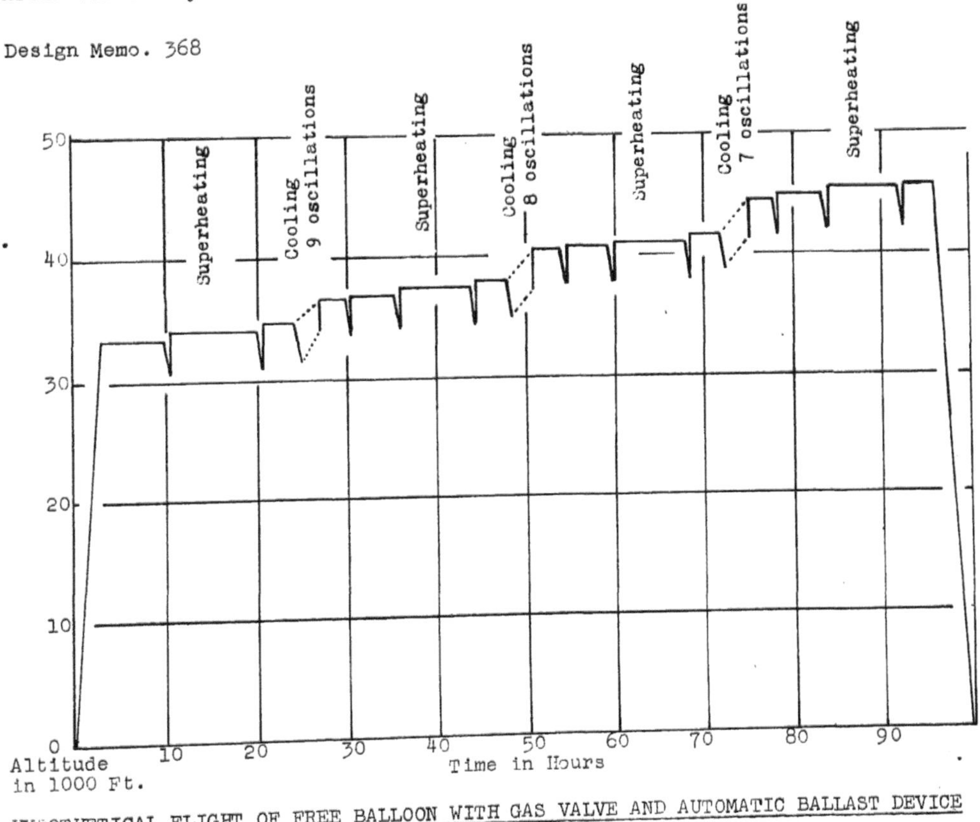

Superheating
Cooling 9 oscillations
Superheating
Cooling 8 oscillations
Superheating
Cooling 7 oscillations
Superheating

50
40
30
20
10
0
Altitude in 1000 Ft.

10 20 30 40 50 60 70 80 90
Time in Hours

HYPOTHETICAL FLIGHT OF FREE BALLOON WITH GAS VALVE AND AUTOMATIC BALLAST DEVICE
ALTITUDE VS TIME

DISTRIBUTION LIST

Sec Nav	1
Asst SecNav	1
Op-16	1
Op-16-B	1
Op-16-PT	1
BuOrd	1
Sonrd	1
Op-34-E	1
Op-31-F	1
LTA Design	1
Naval aide to the President	1
NRL	1
TAIC	1
Comweseafron	5
Army Ground Forces	3
MIS G2	225
Technical Research Library	1
Navy Bomb Disposal School	1
CinCPac	1
Com 3rd Fleet	1
Com 5th Fleet	1
Com 7th Fleet	1
Com South Pacific Area	1
CinCPac-CinCPOA	1
Com Air Force Pac Fleet	1
ComAirPac (Operational Intelligence Section)	1
Com Fleet Air Alameda	1
Com Air 7th Fleet	1
Com Fleet Air Seattle	1
Com Fleet Airships Seattle	1
Com Fleet Airships Pacific	1
Com Support Aircraft Pacific Fleet	1
Com Pac Carrier Transport SF	1
Com Alaska Sea Fron	1
Com East Sea Fron	1
Com Gulf Sea Fron	1
Com Hawaiian Sea Frontier	1
US Naval Adv Int. Center So Pac	1
Com 7th Fleet Int. Center	1
US Naval Adv Int. Center North Pac	1
ComFairWest Coast	1
Room 1W12, Attn: Lt. Poor, Navy Dept.	Balance

www.ingramcontent.com/pod-product-compliance
Ingram Content Group UK Ltd.
Pitfield, Milton Keynes, MK11 3LW, UK
UKHW040559210726
13854UKWH00008B/1643